CHARACTER

MAKES A DIFFERENCE

CHARACTER
MAKES A DIFFERENCE

WHERE I'M FROM • WHERE I'VE BEEN • WHAT I BELIEVE

MIKE HUCKABEE

WITH JOHN PERRY

B&H
PUBLISHING GROUP
NASHVILLE, TENNESSEE

CHARACTER MAKES A DIFFERENCE

© 2007 by Mike Huckabee

All rights reserved

ISBN: 978-0-7394-9289-5

B&H Publishing Group

Nashville, Tennessee

Originally published as:

Character Is the Issue © 1997 by Mike Huckabee

Includes selected chapters from:

Living Beyond Your Lifetime © 2000 by Mike Huckabee

Unless otherwise stated all Scripture citations are from the New King James Version, © 1979, 1980, 1982, Thomas Nelson Publishers, Inc.

Printed in the United States of America

TABLE OF CONTENTS

Part III: Selected Speeches & Commentary

INTRODUCTION

Responding to questions regarding his personal character, President Bill Clinton once told his audience that "character isn't the issue." Yet our character defines the world we live in. Our government, welfare programs, schools, and everything else in our lives are shaped and directed according to our character. It's commonly claimed that "you can't legislate morality," but, in fact, every law in the country is a reflection of our moral values. We have laws against murder and stealing because we believe they are morally wrong. We used to have laws against abortion under most circumstances. When our moral values changed, the laws changed along with them.

Over the past thirty years, a decline in moral character has produced a decline in the character of our society. Columnists and researchers have produced a whole library of books and reports on the issue and laid blame for our cultural troubles on everything from government policy to single parent households. What it all comes down to, though, is that people of good, godly character make good, godly laws. Everything hinges on the character of the men and women we choose to establish public policies.

And their character depends on you.

This is a book for everyone who looks out at the world, sees the moral decline that seems to be devouring our culture unchecked, and thinks, *Our country is falling apart and there's nothing I can do about it.*

There is something you can do about it: you can live a God-centered life of high moral character, and you can run for public office or support candidates who share your Christian standards. At first that sounds like an oversimplification—maybe even an impossibility—but I can tell you from personal experience that it can happen.

I was once the pastor of a wonderful church in Texarkana, Arkansas. We had a growing church, an active television ministry, and a wide-ranging series of community outreach programs. But I felt God's call to leave the pulpit and take my message into the political arena. I had no experience in politics. I was a Republican in a heavily Democratic state. And yet I had a God-centered worldview that my fellow Arkansans identified with.

My views didn't make me any better than anyone else before God, but they struck a chord with people who were weary of living under a government that no longer respected what they thought was important. When I became governor of Arkansas in 1996, I recognized the same moral authority—God's authority—that I did as a pastor, as a student, and as a radio disc jockey in high school. God's standards never change; they are an unmoving goal toward which we can travel all our lives without ever having to change direction.

There are three sections in this book, each dealing with a different aspect of how character shapes the events and institutions of our culture. The first section gives examples of how character can direct the outcome of a crisis. From political showdowns to life-threatening illness, character equips us to face daunting challenges and prevail over them.

The second section focuses on why character is important, how we know there are absolutes of good and bad character, and the consequences of surrendering those absolutes to the champions of relativism.

The final section, comprised of speeches and public commentary, shows how character decisions translate directly into public policy decisions.

Character is the issue, and your character makes a difference every day—in the work you do, the candidates you vote for, the people who look to you for leadership. My hope is that this book will encourage you to live your faith proudly and publicly and to support and uplift fellow Christians as we work together to build God's kingdom.

PART I

CHARACTER IN THE FURNACE

1
A CRUCIBLE MOMENT

My office wasn't the best place in the world to rehearse a speech, but my staff was doing its best to keep interruptions to a minimum. Outside the door, people were running around like members of a pit crew working the Indianapolis 500—fast, efficient, focused, everybody with a job to do, swarming everywhere at once.

It was 1:40 p.m. I wasn't going on the air for several hours, but this was my only opportunity to practice my speech from the TelePrompTer. In twenty minutes I was scheduled to be sworn in as governor of Arkansas. Meetings and other official duties would follow, right up to the time of my live, statewide address at 5:15 p.m.

I had spent days writing and timing this speech; I wanted to make sure everything was just right. (See appendix 1.)

In the relative calm of the capitol office which I had used for almost three years as lieutenant governor, I sat at my desk and read aloud:

> . . . The responsibility that has been thrust upon me and entrusted to me is one that I approach with unapologetic dependence upon the Spirit of God to give me the heart of a servant, wisdom for the difficult decisions I will face each day, the courage to stand by my convictions, and the humility to acknowledge my mistakes, of which there will be many.
>
> A few weeks ago, when a jury of our fellow Arkansans patiently reached a verdict in a nearby federal courthouse, our state was shattered emotionally and politically. My decision to withdraw from the race for the United States Senate and concentrate wholeheartedly on serving you as governor is one I do not regret. I want to help restore Arkansas' image to America as a place of natural beauty, hard-working people, and a family-friendly atmosphere. . . .

Less than two months before, on May 28, 1996, Governor Jim Guy Tucker had been convicted on federal charges of fraud and conspiracy in the first Whitewater trial. Jim and Susan McDougal, principals in Madison Guaranty Savings and Loan, had been convicted the same day. While the McDougals had gotten more national publicity because of their ties to

Governor Tucker's predecessor in office, President Bill Clinton, Tucker's conviction had a far greater effect on the people of Arkansas.

After his conviction was announced, Governor Tucker made a promise to the people of Arkansas that he would resign as governor on or before July 15, 1996. That meant I would move into the governor's office, becoming only the third Republican governor since Reconstruction. At the time, I had a double-digit lead in the race for a seat vacated by popular Democrat David Pryor in the United States Senate but had pulled out of the campaign to concentrate my energies on my duties as governor. Arkansas remained one of the few states whose people had never elected a Republican senator, and if I were to be elected, it would be political history. As it turned out, an even more historic moment was about to occur.

As I continued practicing my speech, friends and staff members walked in and out of the office, some of them talking quietly in a far corner of the room. Monday, July 15, was a brutally hot day in Little Rock. With a dozen or more people in the office, it was getting stuffy despite the air conditioning.

Nearing the end of my script, I looked into the Tele-PrompTer and read: "Being governor of Arkansas is an honor I could never have imagined as a small boy growing up under modest circumstances. I only wish my father could have lived just four more months to have witnessed this day. But somehow, I can't help but believe he's watching all of it from the best seat in the house. When I was fifteen years old, a verse from the New Testament, Philippians 4:13, changed my life. It says, 'I can do all things through Christ who strengthens me.' I'll do my best. And with my family's support, your prayers, and God's help, I can do this job. . . ."

It was 1:55 p.m. The speech timed out perfectly. (Stopwatches held by staff members Gary Underwood and Rex Nelson were within two seconds of fifteen minutes.) Any moment now, a delegation from the state legislature, already in session at the other end of the capitol, would arrive to provide the traditional escort for the governor-elect through the marble corridors and into the House chamber. The official swearing-in would be at 2 p.m., followed by a public ceremony and rally outside on the capitol steps an hour later.

A Disturbing Surprise

I was stretching my legs and talking to Rex, my new communications director, when the phone rang. It was Dawn Cook, my personal secretary, who would be moving with me down the hall into the governor's office. She said Governor Tucker was on the line. I thought he was making a courtesy call to tell me the keys were in the desk and to wish me well. The transition had not been easy, and I was relieved that at this late moment he would have a word of advice or encouragement.

"Hello, Governor," I said when he came on the line. I signaled for quiet in the room and the rumble of conversation stopped.

"Hello, Mike," Tucker began. "I hope everything went okay out at the church."

That morning there had been a prayer and dedication service at First Baptist Church of Little Rock. Some of my pastor friends from my years as a Baptist minister were there, and each one read Scripture or gave a sermon or a charge. Stirring music filled the sanctuary. It was almost like an ordination service, as if every person who spoke made statements that prepared us for the unexpected events of the rest of the day. I will always believe that service was the turning point for me in preparing for a challenge I could never have imagined.

"Yes, it was a very nice service," I responded, thinking that his question seemed odd under the circumstances.

"I'm glad everything went well." He was stalling. Something was up.

After a few seconds of awkward silence, he continued. "Well, I wanted to let you know I've decided not to resign. I filed a motion to appeal on Friday, and until the court rules on it, I feel I should continue in office. I'm going to declare disability and let you serve as acting governor until then. At that time I can make some final disposition."

Not resigning! They were the most unbelievable words I'd ever heard. I signaled for a piece of paper. This was an historic conversation, and I wanted to record both sides of it. Somebody handed me a yellow pad, and I started scribbling as fast as I could. Rex looked at my first words at the top of the page: "Not Resigning!"

To the rest of the people in the room, Rex mouthed silently, "He's not resigning."

I scribbled as Governor Tucker talked. "If my appeal is granted and the verdict is overturned," he told me, "it would be unfair to the people who elected me for me to give up my office."

Brenda Turner, our chief of staff, looked at me with eyes as big as dinner plates. There had been no warning of this. Neither the legislature nor my office had been notified that the governor had changed his mind.

"Governor," I answered, "I'm supposed to take the oath of office in five minutes. The legislative escort is probably waiting outside my door. I respectfully ask that you reconsider this action, not only to keep your word, but for the welfare of the state of Arkansas."

"The people of Arkansas voted for me," he said. "Over four hundred thousand of them elected me governor. They didn't elect you."

This was simply bizarre. He was totally out of touch with reality. I knew a confrontation would be useless, so I tried to steer the conversation toward his place in history and the importance of acting for the good of the state.

"I don't think the people of Arkansas will understand," I told him. "You didn't place any conditions or limitations on your promise to resign, and to go back on that now would very likely be seen as a breach of public trust. Governor, I think that you need to reconsider. The people of Arkansas will think you're going back on your word."

By this time hundreds of spectators had gathered for the ceremony, many of whom had taken a vacation day to be present. A full afternoon and evening of activities had been planned. Even as we spoke, my staff was moving into the governor's office down the hall while Tucker's was moving out. Mine had quit other jobs to join me; many of his staff had lined up new positions and already had made commitments to new employers.

"Governor," I said, "we have people who have left their jobs and sold their homes who are on the job today. And, as you know, members of your staff have moved and have taken other jobs."

"Well, I realize that is going to be a problem," he agreed, "but that's just something that we'll have to work through. Now as far as you're concerned, you can go ahead and move into the governor's mansion. You'll have full use of the house and security staff, and you'll have the salary. And if I need to come back, we will just deal with that."

I couldn't imagine anything more impractical. It was a crazy idea. "Governor," I said, "do you honestly expect me to move my family a hundred and fifty miles up here from Texarkana, move my furniture, get my kids enrolled in school, and then have you decide in six weeks you're going to come back? Does that seem reasonable?"

My wife, Janet, walked up beside me and squeezed my arm. When someone's trying to rewrite your life over the telephone, God's gift of a wonderful spouse is truly a blessing to be treasured. Yet nothing I said could change the governor's mind.

"Well, I'll consider what you said and let you know," he said. I hung up the phone.

A Crisis Looms

"He's not resigning," I announced to those in the room. During the course of a ten-minute conversation, we had moved from a day of celebration to arguably the greatest constitutional crisis in Arkansas history. "We can't let this happen," I declared. "We have to uphold an orderly transfer of power. We cannot let Governor Tucker go back on his promise; we should move forward. Acceptance of this is not an option. If there's anyone who doesn't agree with me on this, speak now or forever hold your peace."

No one spoke.

I turned to Brenda. "We've got to know what our legal options are. See if you can get Leon Holmes in here. He's the best constitutional lawyer in the state. And Frank Arey. And notify Judge Holt." Frank Arey was my new chief legal counsel, while Jack Holt Jr. was the former chief justice of the Arkansas

Supreme Court, a Democrat who had advised us during the transition.

Someone turned on a TV. Live coverage of the ceremony had begun. Pictures of the House chamber filled the screen. State representatives were waiting impatiently, looking at their watches.

It was 2:15 p.m. The legislative escort had been waiting for me about twenty minutes. We told them there had been a short delay and we weren't ready yet. They returned to the legislative chamber empty-handed, knowing something wasn't right, but suspecting we were having trouble ironing out details of the ceremony.

The telephone on my desk rang. The call got cut off somehow, and while the operator was putting it through again, I was handed a letter from the governor. As I opened the envelope, the phone rang a second time. Governor Tucker was on the line. Had I received his letter?

"It was just handed to me. I'm reading it now," I answered.

In the letter he repeated the position he had taken on the phone. He was declaring himself disabled and temporarily "unable to discharge the duties of the Office of Governor," according to provisions in the state constitution. "This decision to declare an inability to serve," the letter read, "arises from the discovery just last week that goes to the heart of my citizen's right to receive a fair trial from an impartial jury."

A member of the Whitewater jury that convicted him, he explained, married a prisoner who had once petitioned the governor to commute his forty-year sentence for cocaine possession. The governor had refused. This, he claimed, had prejudiced the juror against him. "I expect the court to grant a hearing on this issue and decide this matter prior to August 19, 1996. If the verdict is set aside, it eliminates the reason for my decision to resign. . . ."

Now he told me he had been considering our earlier conversation. "I thought this over," he said. "It's clear to me what I should do, and my mind is made up. I'm going to declare disability. I will effectively now turn the controls of government over to you and, after this is resolved in August, I will make a final disposition. I expect that I will be fully exonerated and will resume the duties of governor at that time."

"How will you handle the announcement to the House and Senate as well as to the public?" I asked. He had sent the legislature the same note I had received, he said, and he considered that sufficient. "This can be an easy transition or a hard one," he continued. "It all depends on you." I replied that I respectfully disagreed. That decision was in his court, not mine.

The News Spreads

Meanwhile on television, House parliamentarian Tim Massanelli was reading a copy of the governor's letter to a dumbfounded legislature and the hundreds of guests who had crowded into the chamber for the ceremony. The buzz of voices rose steadily as the letter was read. When Mr. Massanelli looked up from the page after reading the last word, the buzz became a roar. The state supreme court justices stood and filed out of the chamber.

Many of the old-time Democrats all but fell on the floor and ripped their garments in twain. It had been bad enough to have a Democratic governor leave office after being convicted on felony charges. But then to have him pull this stunt in a state where honor means so much was almost more than they could bear. Keeping your word is a sacred thing in Arkansas. My dad used to say, "The only thing a poor man has is his word. It's the one thing nobody can take from you." It looked as if our governor had given his away.

Though I didn't know it then, Governor Tucker called a news conference just after our phone conversation. "If I am to resign, there should be a reason," he told the press assembled in the high-ceilinged governor's conference room. "The elimination of the verdict would eliminate the reason for my announced resignation. I regret if it causes anyone any inconvenience, but I expect this will be as smooth and orderly as those involved wish to make it. I'm sure there will be those who will want to have a fight and disagree about it. If that's what they choose to do, that's how it will have to be."

The governor and his wife, Betty, then left the capitol, surrounded by a protective cordon of state police. Word of his decision had spread to the huge crowd outside. Sight of him prompted an immediate, raw, visceral reaction—people booed, screamed, and shouted, "Liar!" "How could you?" "You're a disgrace!" On reading the newspaper account later, I felt so sorry for this man and his wife. There was no joy, no benefit to anyone, in their tragic decision.

After my second phone conversation with the governor, I looked around at my staff members and friends filling the office. "One man's misjudgment is not going to jeopardize the future of two and a half million Arkansans," I declared. "I want us to move forward with dignity. I want it done right. But on the other hand, this is one of those crucible moments in the history of this state. If we allow this sort of outrageous indifference to promises, to the laws of this state, and to the people of this state, then we are responsible."

"Can you accept legal responsibility for this?" someone asked.

"I don't see how we cannot accept legal responsibility," I answered.

It wasn't a matter of politics or parties or careers. It was a matter of Governor Tucker keeping his oath to the people of Arkansas, and of me keeping mine. If people were determined to think I was going after the governor for my own benefit, so be it.

The legislature and the people had to be reassured that the office of the governor was being safeguarded, that the lines of responsibility and command were clear, even in this time of crisis. Reporters wanted to know who was in control of the National Guard. The state police had to know who the governor's security detail was supposed to protect.

I told those in my office that I thought I should address the legislature if the governor would not. Several of them suggested that I wait until my scheduled television address at 5:15 p.m., a little more than two and a half hours away. I thought momentarily of my carefully rehearsed speech—now worthless—and wondered what I would say instead.

"I don't think we should wait that long," I said. "The citizens of Arkansas need to know what's going on. If there's a question we can't answer, we'll be honest and say we don't know." I took the position that I had assumed the responsibilities of governor at noon, the time Tucker had set for his resignation. Until legal counsel or the courts said otherwise, that would be our view.

It was a controversial decision. As discussion continued, more staff members voiced their opposition to my facing the legislature in person. I was thinking, *I can either leave it up to Tucker—because he is the one who has made them angry—or I can go down there and speak to them myself and try to salvage the situation.*

Finally I said, "I do not want to hide out or crawl under the table. I think I should tell the legislature we can accept this letter and let one person guide our destiny, or we can stand together and explore our options."

Once I made up my mind, I was very firm about my decision. I resolved to go face-to-face with the legislature and take charge. Governor Tucker's actions were unacceptable. His decision-making ability was clearly impaired, and I had to demonstrate to the legislature that we had to stand together and take action for the good of the state. The governor was disabled, but not just temporarily. He was incapable of discharging the responsibilities of his office.

Rex went into the hallway to answer what questions he could. Releasing what little information we could would be better than allowing the rumor mill to get cranking.

"Does Governor Huckabee's staff have a budget?" a reporter asked.

"No," Rex replied. "We're all working as volunteers until further notice."

"Who has the powers of office at this moment?"

"Acting Governor Huckabee has been given the powers of office, according to the state constitution. He's meeting with advisors now to look at how best to proceed." Whether those official powers were permanent or temporary remained to be seen.

"What about all the receptions and other activities planned for tonight?"

"They're still on, as scheduled. And Acting Governor Huckabee will still make his statewide address at 5:15."

A Humbling Moment

A little before 3 p.m., an Arkansas State Police security detail, assisted by Capitol Police officers, escorted Janet, the children (John Mark, 20; David, 16; and Sarah, 13), members of the staff, and me to the House chamber. The security team cleared a path in the hallway outside my office, and we opened the door. The enormous, elegant hall was packed shoulder-to-shoulder with well-wishers who started clapping and cheering, their shouts echoing off the bright white marble walls. All the way up the marble staircase to the House, the crowd lined both balustrades, parting far enough only to let the officers by, with the rest of us following in a compacted clump behind them. Sarah lost her place behind the police and was swallowed up in the crowd. Several people fell back to rescue her. Unable to work their way back to us, they returned to my office to watch the proceedings on television.

As we approached the huge, ornate double doors with "HOUSE" carved in the marble overhead, citizens jamming the stairs and hallway and spilling out onto the sidewalk around the capitol began to chant, their voices increasing in volume and intensity, "We want Mike! We want Mike! We want *Mike!* We want MIKE!" As soon as the doors to the chamber were opened, an enormous swell of cheers and applause cascaded out, roiling with the noise in the hallway. The commotion was so loud that we couldn't hear the doorkeeper announce us to the Speaker. After a moment, Janet and I walked to our place on the dais through a sea of standing, jumping, exuberant people, some of them waving with both hands.

It was one of the most humbling moments of my life (and as clear an example as I ever expect to see of God's divine providence working in my life). It wasn't my political skills or anything else of my own doing that had brought me to this moment. Only God could have done this.

Bobby Hogue, Speaker of the House, called for order and the turmoil began to subside. My good friend Roy Parker, pastor of Beech Street First Baptist Church, the church I had once pastored in Texarkana, offered a short prayer. After the Pledge of Allegiance, I was introduced as "Lieutenant Governor Mike Huckabee, acting governor of the great state of Arkansas." The roar of applause erupted again as I stood and walked to the podium. After a moment it grew quiet enough for me to speak. The atmosphere was electric. Supercharged.

"Is there something going on here this afternoon that I need to know about?" I asked.

As I had hoped, my question broke the tension. Laughter rippled through the auditorium, then silence. I glanced at the single sheet of notes I had hurriedly prepared and went on. I had been tempted to send a written message to the chamber, but decided to speak directly to them. And so I began: "I've chosen to come and speak to you face-to-face and heart-to-heart."

That remark brought more cheers. Though I appreciated the response, I suggested that the listeners hold their applause, considering the seriousness of the occasion. I recapped the information outlined in the letter we all had just received. "This is a very critical moment in our state's history," I said, "and it demands that our response be measured only by how effectively we as elected officials act with the caliber of calm yet courage required for such a moment in our history. I would like to request an immediate meeting with the Speaker of the House and the president pro tempore of the Senate. . . ."

I added that I would still address the state at 5:15 p.m. and at that time would report on our meeting to all the citizens of the state, including public officials "who, with me, have been elected to stand tall in a moment like this . . . to represent not what we think or what we hope or believe, but to represent the heart, the mind, and the very essence of the people who put us in these sacred positions of trust."

The chamber roared with applause as Janet and I stepped down from the podium. That was the turning point of the day. I doubt the legislature expected me to exhibit such a clear direction and firm hand. We were calm but resolved. Our team showed a strong focus. Nobody was overly excited, which was amazing. Nobody panicked. We had a job to do, and we were going to do it. It was orderly and methodical.

Crucial Steps

A few minutes later we were sitting in my office with Speaker Bobby Hogue and Senate President Pro Tempore Stanley Russ. We had to make important decisions quickly, in a spirit of unity. We couldn't begin with ambivalence.

"Here is the situation," I told them. "What is happening here is completely unacceptable. The people of this state are looking to us for leadership. They need to know their state is under control. What the governor has done is outrageous and unacceptable. It is a betrayal of the public trust, and we have got to make it very clear that this isn't going to work."

Bobby and Stanley were two experienced, capable Democratic legislators in the most lopsidedly Democratic state legislature in the country. I doubt they ever expected to hear words like that from a Republican acting governor.

I said to Bobby, "A lot of people are going to want to blame, not Jim Guy Tucker, but you and the Democratic Party. They're ready to believe this is a conspiracy. I know that's not true. I believe that you are as shocked as I am about what he has done. I believe that this is the act of a single individual and not of the party. I am willing to stand with you publicly to defend your honor with this, but I expect you to stand with me publicly as I take us through these next few hours.

"It is not my intention to hurt Governor Tucker or the Democratic Party. It is simply our goal to move on. Really, his only options are to resign or to have us call for his impeachment. I have a televised address in less than two hours. The time is reserved, and I *will* be talking to the people of Arkansas. You need to talk to Governor Tucker and tell him that if he will resign unconditionally before five o'clock this afternoon, then we will never use the word 'impeachment.' We'll just let it be that he has reconsidered, has resigned as he promised to do, and there will never be any other discussion about it. But if he does not resign by five o'clock, at 5:15 p.m. I will be on the air and I will call for his impeachment. I will announce that we are in the process of preparing the necessary papers, that I am calling the General Assembly into a special session Wednesday for the purpose of beginning impeachment proceedings. He needs to know that I am resolved in this." They agreed to talk with him about it.

I then left for the Excelsior Hotel downtown to change and shave in preparation for the telecast. While there, I got a call from Hogue and Russ with news I didn't want to hear: the governor had no intention of resigning.

2
A DELICATE VESSEL

It was time for my television address to be broadcast from my office. A TV crew covered the windows with black paper and set up its lights and cameras. I took my place in a chair in the middle of the room. The TelePrompTer was in position—but revealed only a blank screen. Three and a half hours earlier in the same room, I had rehearsed a speech carefully crafted for the occasion. It seemed like a year ago. And history had sent that script straight to the trash can.

"Thirty seconds to air."

I felt no sense of discomfort or apprehension. I would say what I knew was right for our state, what God had put in my heart.

"Ten seconds and counting. . . . Five seconds. . . . Cue."

Tonight I stand before you with no script, with no written words, just a few moments to share with you from the depths of my heart as a fellow Arkansas citizen exactly where we are in this very critical moment in our state's history. . . . What really is at issue tonight is a simple question between right and wrong. This afternoon, I spent a lot of time listening to legal counsel—wise and experienced people of the law. There are as many opinions as there are lawyers, as you know. But as this hour approached, I realized that this is not the time for a committee decision. What we have to do is come to a place where we take clear and decisive action because, frankly, that is what you have elected us to do. . . .

I tried very diligently to be cooperative and to be quiet about the actions of the past seven weeks—the hundreds of appointments, the nearly $58 million in state money. [Between the May 28 verdict and July 15, the governor had made more than three hundred political appointments—including 174 in a single day!—and spent almost $58 million.] I remained silent because the governor was still the governor until a court said he was not. . . . We never imagined the governor would make any kind of decision like this. . . .

We received the letters indicating his refusal to step down. . . . There are many who will probably say this is going to be great for the Republicans. My friends, this is simply going to be bad for all of us. No Republican could ever take pleasure in what has happened, nor should any Democrat be branded with the responsibility of it. . . .

The governor has been notified that as of nine o'clock in the morning, if we have not received from him a letter of unreserved and unqualified resignation, a proclamation which is being prepared even as I speak will be signed and put into motion first thing in the morning. That proclamation will call for an immediate, emergency session of the General Assembly. We will ask the members of the Arkansas House and Senate to convene on Wednesday morning at ten o'clock for the purpose of initiating the process of impeachment and ultimately the removal from office of Jim Guy Tucker as governor of Arkansas. . . .

If there are court challenges, let them come. We're more than ready to face them. If there are challenges from those who write columns or make opinions, let them come. We have not been elected to take a poll or check with opinion writers, or even to be threatened with legal action. We have been elected to serve you and represent you. . . .

Here is what I pledge to you. I'll make my share of mistakes. Always have, always will. That is why I am grateful to God that He is a God who looks at us— with all He knows about us—and still loves us, still forgives us, still empowers us to go on. Now there are those who tell me, "Mike, don't make so many quotes from the Bible in your speeches." Well, a word to those who would perhaps, with good intentions, tell me not to reference God or the Bible. The fact is that since my childhood, that Book and its Author have been the guiding forces in my life. And it would be much easier for me to give up being governor than it would be to give up taking the counsel that I have had from God and His Word.

Now I very much hope and trust that each one of you as Arkansas citizens will let your desires be known to your representative and your state senator. You elected them to represent you, and I believe these are honorable men and women. Don't think that the Democratic representatives don't feel equally embarrassed. Don't think that they have some agenda here other than what is best for Arkansas. Call them. Let them know tonight and tomorrow your feelings and desires. And let us all pray that Governor Tucker will do the right thing for Arkansas, for the Tuckers, and for Arkansas history.

Finally the TV lights went off and somebody took the black paper off the windows. "Nobody will ever believe you didn't have a script," the cameraman said.

Let the words of my mouth . . . be acceptable in Your sight, O Lord . . . (Psalm 19:14).

After the speech, I learned that State Attorney General Winston Bryant was already setting the legal wheels in motion. He had announced his intention to file suit in circuit court to have Governor Tucker removed from office and was urging lawmakers to consider impeachment.

Bryant was in a tough spot because he faced criticism no matter what he did, whether he supported the governor or opposed him. He was the Democratic nominee for the U.S. Senate race in November and would have run against me had I not dropped out to assume the duties of governor. Nonpartisan polls had me more than fifteen points ahead. If Bryant pressed for Tucker's removal, he would be accused of trying to take out Tucker so I would become governor, drop out of the Senate race, and make it easier for Bryant to win.

Legally, though, there was a big question whether Tucker could remain in office as a convicted felon. Some accused Bryant of being too chummy with the governor and too protective of Democratic Party turf. Tucker's political appointments and runaway spending after May 28 were legally suspect, but Bryant had chosen to leave the issue alone. "Well, we don't really know what we should do," he'd say.

Yet suddenly, on the afternoon of July 15, he declared he was going to file a lawsuit in the morning and challenge the legality of Tucker's remaining in office. Bryant could see that the train was about to leave the station, and he wanted to be on board. I've kidded him about it since, but in all fairness, he didn't have a lot of options.

The Second Letter

After the television address, we set up an impromptu news conference in the hallway outside my office. I had answered only a few questions when Rex came out, interrupted me, and called me back inside. We had just received a second letter from Governor Tucker: "The Republican lieutenant governor has informed me that he intends to call a special session of the General Assembly. I hereby notify you that my inability to serve as governor has ended, and I have resumed the powers of the office of governor as of 4:40 p.m., July 15, 1996."

Again, we huddled in my office to discuss our options. The lines of authority could get confused quickly unless we took decisive action. I carried Governor Tucker's two letters to me back into the hallway where the reporters and others were waiting. I read the second letter, in which the governor claimed his inability to serve had ended. Then I read part of the first, where he described his inability to serve as being caused by his felony convictions currently under appeal.

"His inability has not ended," I pointed out. "His appeal is still pending, and he still needs to honor his promise to resign today without qualification."

The second letter reopened the question of exactly who was governor at the moment. Who should the governor's security detail protect? Who commanded the National Guard? My stance was unwavering: "You follow my orders. You have to make a choice, but I am expecting you to follow mine."

At that point everything fell apart for the governor and his allies. The Democratic leadership had done its best to help him work his way out of this mess, but when he tried to reclaim the reins of power, even his closest friends began to distance themselves from him.

All of us, Democrats and Republicans, were pulling together for a common good. We realized that we had to make decisions thoughtfully. We had to do it right because we would have no opportunity to do it over.

Once more I affirmed that I held the duties and responsibilities of governor until a court ruled otherwise. I encouraged everyone to call their state representatives and senators. It would be their decision whether to accept Tucker's demands or vote to begin impeachment proceedings.

I think we all sensed the gravity of the day. The Arkansas Constitution at that moment was a delicate vessel that had been placed in our hands, and we were responsible for seeing that it was not dropped and shattered, but rather that we handed back to the people a stable, secure government that had their full confidence.

News of the crisis had worked its way down the street to the federal building, where the *New York Times* and other national press were covering a Whitewater trial. It was a slow day there, and many of the out-of-state reporters left the federal courthouse to join the Arkansas press corps at the capitol. The whole country would be watching to see how the state and its leaders responded. What would happen?

Even in this crisis, the ultimate decision was in the hands of the citizens. If they insisted on Tucker's return, their representatives in the General Assembly would vote against the resolution to impeach. If they were willing to accept my leadership, they could call their legislators and say so.

Over at the offices of the *Arkansas Democrat-Gazette*, the switchboard lit up like the Fourth of July as citizens called to get the names of their districts' senators and representatives.

The tension of the situation had prompted the head of the state police to station thirty or forty state troopers at the capitol and have another thirty or forty standing by. Everybody they could get into uniform was on duty. Even Jim Clark, who runs the crime lab, was standing guard.

In the hall at the capitol, Speaker Hogue spoke briefly to reporters. He said he had talked with Governor Tucker and that he had stood with him through a lot but could stand with him no more. He had advised the governor to resign and would support a motion for impeachment on Wednesday. It took a great deal of courage to stand in front of the national press and take sides against a governor of his own party. But as I had said a few minutes earlier on the air, this was no time for Democrats and Republicans to draw sides; it was a time to draw together.

The Crisis Subsides

As I was answering one reporter's question, a radio corre-
spondent holding a cell phone interrupted me. "Our newsroom
is saying they've just gotten word that Tucker has resigned," he
announced.

"Governor," Rex quickly interjected, "we best go inside
and get some information." I went back into the office to
chase down this latest rumor. It didn't take long to uncover the
facts. Tucker had, in fact, decided to resign. Sharon Priest, the
Arkansas secretary of state, had traveled to Democratic Party
headquarters to receive his resignation letter. She drove back to
the capitol, parked her car, and was climbing the steps. Larry
Audas, a news anchor for Channel 11, a Little Rock station
broadcasting live, stuck a microphone in her face and said,
"Ms. Priest, any new developments?"

"Well," she answered, "I've got this resignation here in my
hand from Governor Tucker."

What a scoop!

Larry read the letter on the air, a handwritten note on official governor's mansion stationery, addressed to the president
pro tempore of the senate. "Dear Mr. President: This is to
inform you that I hereby resign the office of governor effective
at 6 p.m., July 15, 1996."

When word of the resignation reached the reporters and
others standing in the hall, a roar of applause thundered
through the vast marble area. I don't think it was the sound of

political victory, because politics weren't the issue. Character was the issue; the resolve to do right, regardless of the circumstances or of the consequences, was the issue. It was the sound of relief, of thanksgiving, of celebration, that we had prevailed together in a crisis.

What Jim Guy Tucker had unintentionally done was to give the new administration the emotional mandate of the people. He also gave us the opportunity to show we could handle pressure. It might have taken months or years to prove those things in the course of handling routine state business. But from the first hour, nobody who knew the facts could say we were inept lightweights, caretakers, or lame ducks.

The swearing-in ceremony was rescheduled for 6:45 that evening. Busloads of friends from across the state, who had waited all afternoon to see what would happen, filed back into the House chamber. Speaker Hogue called the session to order, and this time the ceremony went off exactly as planned. With my hand on a green leather Bible, which Janet held, I took the oath of office from the chief justice of the Arkansas Supreme Court. In a few brief remarks, I said again that I hoped no one would see this as an opportunity for gloating or political posturing. It was time to put this sad episode behind us and get on with the business of making Arkansas an even better place to live.

The caterers at the convention center had been keeping vigil, hoping the cakes that said "Congratulations Governor Huckabee" wouldn't end up an embarrassment. The party started a little late, but the cakes fit right in. Finally, I could celebrate and thank all the people who had worked so hard during the seven weeks of transition, supporters who had been so efficient and clearheaded during this long day of crisis.

The day proved to me that when everybody shares the view that *right* and *truth* are not relative conditions, but absolutes, you don't have to spend a lot of time explaining what to do and why. A few clear, immovable milestones made the day's decisions easy. We couldn't let the irrational decisions of one person control the destiny of Arkansas; that would have been wrong. We couldn't worry about the opinion makers and naysayers; if we were resolved to do right, their opinions were irrelevant. We couldn't fret about the political or legal liabilities we might have incurred; they were simply part of the cost of sticking to our moral guns.

Some people don't believe in moral absolutes and the power of integrity. I would challenge them to chart a successful path through a *real* crisis with an untested team using any other standards. I don't think it can be done.

Late that night back at the Excelsior Hotel, where we were to stay until we could occupy the governor's mansion, I kept replaying the events of that historic and bizarre day. How could someone with the political savvy and experience of Jim Guy Tucker do what he had done?

Perhaps the bitterness and resentment he felt as a result of his conviction grew to the point that they got the upper hand. In the end, he had unintentionally done me a favor.

On the morning of July 15, plenty of people thought I was an untested, bomb-throwing, right-wing, Christian fundamentalist Republican who would assume a caretaker position until a real governor could be elected. By the end of the day, I felt an overwhelming majority of citizens wanted me to succeed. It had been a long day, and at last it was over.

But the surprises weren't.

3
THE PEOPLE RULE

My first full day as governor got off to a much better start than my first day as lieutenant governor. For one thing, my office door wasn't nailed shut from the inside.

When I had arrived at the capitol as the newly elected lieutenant governor in 1993, the door to my office seemed to be jammed or blocked. I couldn't get it open. It didn't take long to figure out that the door had been nailed shut all the way around the frame from the inside.

"We're going to use the room for the Martin Luther King Jr. Commission," I was told, even though the commission hadn't yet started its work. I couldn't get a straight answer about what was going on. I also couldn't get my door open. It stayed that way for fifty-nine days. John Fund, an editorial writer from

The Wall Street Journal, heard about the incident and flew all the way to Little Rock to see for himself.

As lieutenant governor, it took me four months to get office letterhead. Every time I sent in a requisition, it was returned because it had the "wrong department number" on it, or the "old number," or an "invalid number," or "too many numbers." I finally had to have the lieutenant governor's letterhead printed at my own expense.

Shell-shocked

My first day as governor, I had no problems with insubordination; the predicament was exactly the opposite. Administrative support people who had stayed over from the previous administration were shell-shocked and exhausted. Many of them had not submitted their résumés for consideration by the incoming senior staff. I found out later they hadn't bothered doing so because they had been told they all would be fired and that submitting their résumés was a waste of time. We immediately encouraged them to reapply for their jobs if they wanted to and assured them they would be given fair consideration.

Traditionally, the matter of who will stay and who will go is settled well before a new governor begins his term. Senior policy advisers and staff generally follow the departing governor out of office, but mid-level staff and support personnel sometimes stay on. Yet except for one or two brief encounters between May 28 and July 15, Governor Tucker had refused to discuss the transition process. There had been no meetings on personnel and no discussion of records management, nor the orderly transfer of information regarding state business.

In fact, on my first day as governor, there was no information to transfer. In office after office, we found filing cabinets completely empty. Enough files to fill whole rooms had been shredded or otherwise destroyed. The hard disks on every computer had been erased. We had no records of legislation, no personnel files, no financial records, no accounting ledgers, no correspondence files. Nothing.

Gary Underwood immediately organized a team to rebuild our database. Gary had been on my staff when I was a church pastor and helped our congregation build a community television channel. He supervised the collection of everything we needed to keep the office running without any significant interruption. It wasn't what I had expected to be doing our first day on the job, but the entire office—new hires and veterans alike—pitched in to get the job done.

I also received a gracious letter that day from Jim Guy Tucker:

> I want to publicly apologize to Mike Huckabee and to the people of Arkansas. It was wrong and inconsiderate of me to have changed my resignation schedule as I sought to do yesterday. It was a total surprise to a public who has been wonderfully patient and always trusted

my word. It sullied the day Mike and his supporters had spent weeks planning and had deserved to enjoy. It surprised legislators and upset what had been a generally smooth transition. I apologize and hope Governor Huckabee as well as our good citizens will accept my sincere regrets.

Rebuilding the files in the days that followed was a lot easier than rebuilding morale. In talking with experienced members of the governor's office staff, it was clear that the work atmosphere these people had endured was nothing to smile about.

One of my points of agreement with Franklin D. Roosevelt was his belief that profanity is not the language of a democracy. In order to help improve the spirit of the office, I immediately banned smoking and swearing in the governor's office, not because I'm a self-righteous prude, but because those things kill morale and sap productivity. Everyone, from the most senior staff member to entry-level clerks, deserves courtesy and respect on the job. Cursing at them and blowing smoke in their faces won't do. I also made it clear that I have no patience with people who make sexually inappropriate remarks. What is innocent fun and joking to one person can be uncomfortable or threatening to another.

Longtime staffers in the governor's office were used to being yelled at. I explained that my guiding principle of management leadership is the Golden Rule: Do unto others as you would have them do unto you. If someone makes a mistake and it really upsets him, there is no purpose in my getting upset, too, because he is probably going to be upset enough for both of us. As long as he has learned from it and can move on, my response is, "Let's correct it, let's not repeat it, but let's not kill anybody over it."

The only time I get really upset is when someone makes a mistake that affects me or others but he doesn't care that it does—he's cavalier about it. But otherwise, you can't let mistakes cripple people. Rather than chew their heads off, show them how they can do a better job next time. It's my policy never, ever, to chew someone out in front of others. The only time to pull rank and remind people you're in charge is when someone directly challenges the authority that you and you alone have. That is more than an act of insubordination; it is an act of treason and you have to address it immediately and firmly.

Other than that instance, a person who announces to everyone that he's in charge only proves that he's *not* in charge. A leader who is really in charge never has to mention the fact. His authority is based on respect more than anything else. You can't order people to respect you. Your position may put people in a place where they have to do what you say—but do they comply because they want to, or because they have to? If people follow my orders only because they have to, they will do the bare minimum. If they respond because they want to—because I treat them the way I'd like to be treated—they're happier, more thorough, more encouraging to others, and always looking for ways to do the job better. In other words, the Golden Rule is good for business.

I found out there were governors before me who had never met the people who worked for them. One staff member told me that after she had worked for a particular governor for two years, she happened to see him at a mall. The governor introduced himself and she said, "Governor, I've worked for you the past two years." He didn't even know who she was!

Now, I don't know all of the people in state government, but if they work for me, I want to know who they are. I began walking around to various parts of the capitol, meeting workers in their offices, introducing myself, looking at pictures of their children, and getting to know them a little.

I'm Not the Boss

The changes we made in the office created incredible improvements in the working environment. Once the office staff knew they would be respected, that every job was important, that honest mistakes would be forgiven, that someone cared who they were and what they did, the fears and confusion melted away. It didn't take weeks; it was more a matter of days or even hours. Before the first week was out, staffers from the previous administration were working alongside people who had been my friends for twenty years, with no distinction, no social pecking order, and no baggage from the past.

We were well equipped and well inspired to get on with the people's business.

That phrase "the people's business" suggests perhaps the most important point I made to my staff: I didn't like being called "boss." I thought of us as a team, and I encouraged my coworkers to do the same. Of course, the executive branch of the state government must have a chain of command, and ours does. But part of my job was to reaffirm that every job on the staff was important.

So who is "the boss" in state government? The Arkansas state motto, emblazoned on our official seal, is *Regnat Populus*, which is Latin for "The People Rule." The boss is not the governor but the citizens he serves. On the wall behind my receptionist's desk hung a picture frame with the words "Our Boss" at the top. Every few weeks we put in a different photo. One week it might be a Girl Scout Troop from Arkadelphia; the next week it might be a teacher in Mount Ida; the next week, a retired farmer in West Memphis. These were the people we had pledged to serve. All of us passed this picture frame several times a day. It was an effective reminder of our ultimate place in the chain of command.

The same principle held true when people came to see me. If they came in with tattered clothes and smelled bad and clearly had little power and dignity, the one place where they would be respected was in my office. I have no tolerance for those who look down on others. Some folks may make less money than others; they may live in less adequate houses, or they may have poor job skills—but those in state government are their employees.

A big part of dealing with people is to treat others as you would have them treat you. If you don't want people yelling at you, don't yell at people. If you don't want to be betrayed by people, don't betray others. If you don't like being laughed at, don't laugh at others. I believe in servant leadership. And servant leadership means not cracking the whip.

Servant leadership is the highest form of leadership. It's not the same as doormat leadership. To see your role as servant leader is the ultimate biblical model of leadership. I expected our employees to treat others the way *they* wanted to be treated, to understand that their job was not to be served but to serve— that they were never to be rude. The people out there who called, wrote, or visited were not our problem, irritation, or interruption; they were our *job*. Our challenge was not to get those people out of the way so that we could do our work; our work was to help those people. Those people are citizens of the state, and they are our bosses.

Regnat Populus.

4
IS GOD A DEMOCRAT?

Before being elected lieutenant governor in July 1993, I had spent twelve years as a Baptist pastor: the first six at Immanuel Baptist Church in Pine Bluff, then another six at Beech Street First Baptist Church in Texarkana. When people hear this, they invariably ask how I could have gone from the pulpit into politics. But I think my life was always headed for politics, although for a time it was diverted to the pastorate.

As a teenager, I was far more interested in politics or broadcasting than in the ministry. Even after I left Southwestern Baptist Theological Seminary in Fort Worth, I didn't see myself headed into a pastorate but into a ministry in communications or something else outside the traditional pastoral role.

I had been in the advertising business in Fort Worth after college and seminary but had been preaching since I was fifteen. One Sunday in 1980, I was invited to speak at Immanuel Church in Pine Bluff. The church invited me back to hold a revival, then asked me to serve as its interim pastor and then to stay on permanently. I spent six good years there before accepting a call from Beech Street First Baptist.

My ministry in Pine Bluff was unconventional because my background was in communications, not traditional ministry. So rather than have a typical visitation program, we advertised on bus benches. I did a radio program each day—"Positive Alternatives"—that was designed to be more motivational and inspirational than it was religious. We launched a television channel in Pine Bluff and another station in Texarkana that focused more on local community concerns than on religious ones. We included religious programming, but we also covered high school football and featured talk shows about community events.

It was during this time of ministry that I was gaining maturity and knowledge I would need for a life in public service.

Politics in the Church

Whoever said "politics and religion don't mix" was not a regular churchgoer. I soon discovered that there is an amazing amount of politics in church.

In 1989 I was elected president of the Arkansas Baptist State Convention, the youngest in its 150-year history. With

490,000 members, it is the largest organization of any kind in the state. During my two years as president, the Southern Baptist denomination was undergoing a dramatic change. Traditional, conservative leaders succeeded their more liberal predecessors, and in the process the two sides displayed some of the most intense hardball politics I have ever seen. Some of it was far more brutal than secular politics, in part because in secular politics you *expect* deception and backstabbing; whereas in church politics the common belief is that people are going to behave like Jesus. When they behave more like Beelzebub, you're stunned. In church politics, you're surprised when people are bad, while in secular politics you're surprised when people are good.

In retrospect, I believe Baptist politics paved the way for my later political campaigns. As head of the largest organized group in the state during a tumultuous time, I had the benefit of a lot of media attention. That exposure opened doors for me that wouldn't have opened otherwise, attracting the attention of state Republican Party leaders who expressed an interest in me as a candidate.

I had first gotten interested in the Republicans when I was in high school. I was thirteen in 1968, but I could already tell I was much more in agreement with the conservative Republican viewpoint than I was with Hubert Humphrey's liberalism. By 1972, I was a true-blue, conservative, family-oriented young Republican.

Still, I didn't get involved in party politics while serving as a pastor. I would go to some political dinners or give the invocation at political events, but that was as far as my involvement went. I was certainly open about my personal views, but I never tried to lobby other people in public.

During the time I was president of the Arkansas Baptist State Convention, a couple of my Republican friends asked if I had ever considered running for public office. One of them was Jonathan Barnett. We had met at Boys State (a statewide program for high school boys, designed to encourage interest in civic involvement) in 1972, and were both recruited by the state Republican Party to help in the Nixon campaign. I became the southern Arkansas youth coordinator, while he was my counterpart in the northwest. We stayed in contact through the years. I went on to Ouachita Baptist University in Arkadelphia and to seminary in Fort Worth, while he went to John Brown University in Siloam Springs.

Jonathan ran for state representative when he was eighteen. Even though he lost, the campaign whetted his appetite for politics. "Someday you're going to run for governor, and I'll help you get elected," he told me a little later.

We first discussed the U.S. Senate race early in 1991. I had been growing restless and frustrated in the ministry, asking more and more what there was of significant, eternal value resulting from all the work the church was doing and all the money it was spending. I could point to some accomplishments, but was the output worth the input?

In my early years of ministry, I was quite idealistic, thinking that most people in the congregation expected me to be the captain of a warship leading God's troops into battle to change the world. As the years passed, I became increasingly convinced that most people wanted me to captain the Love Boat, making sure everyone was having a good time. Too many people seemed unconcerned about how many marriages were salvaged, how many kids got off drugs, or how many teen pregnancies were prevented. Rather, the chief concerns seemed to be whether the menus for Wednesday night dinners were appetizing, what color the softball jerseys would be, how loud some guest musicians might sing, whether the coffeepot was ready in the Sunday school building, and whether there were paper towels in the women's rest room.

I grew increasingly frustrated. I wasn't bitter or angry; I just wanted my life to count for something more than being an ordained cruise director. In the U.S. Senate, I thought, a person could make a significant contribution in deciding issues that affect the entire world.

I had to decide whether I would walk away from a comfortable income and career. As a pastor I was set for life. I was pastoring a 2,500-member church at age thirty-five. I had a television ministry (the church had its own studio and transmission tower). I had a generous salary, good benefits, an excellent retirement package—all in all, I probably had more expendable income than I did as governor (I certainly didn't go into politics for the money).

My wife and I had long talks about what to do. Janet and I were married after our freshman year at Ouachita when we were just eighteen. In all the years since, she has been my best friend and confidante. One night, after struggling for weeks about what to do, we took a long walk around our neighborhood, talking and trying to sort things out. If the goal of being a Christian was to be comfortable, we had arrived. But was that where we were supposed to stay? Could I simply say, "I'm a believer" and then kick back and take the world as it came? Jesus told us to be salt and light so our lives might have some kind of impact that will improve the world.

We made our decision that night. The following Sunday, I announced my plans to resign from the ministry, effective the first Sunday in February.

Senator Dale Bumpers would be up for re-election in 1992. He had been governor when I was governor of Boys State in 1972. In fact, he had told me then, "You know, we need young men like you in politics. I hope you will consider that some day." (I quoted his words in speeches when I ran against him.) He had come out of the little town of Charleston, Arkansas, and was considered a fresh face, a young crusader for reform.

Bumpers made a good governor. He had been able to pass legislation stalled for four years by stubborn Democrats because it was proposed by his predecessor, Winthrop Rockefeller, the first Republican elected governor since Reconstruction. Bumpers defeated J. William Fulbright in the 1974 Senate race and went to Washington as a moderate southern Democrat.

Bumpers won by convincing the voters that Fulbright was too liberal and that "we need someone with our values." Oddly enough, Bumpers became increasingly liberal once he went to Washington.

Still, whether I could beat an incumbent Democratic senator as a Republican newcomer was a big question, regardless of the man's record. With few exceptions, including the term of Governor Frank White in 1981–82, the Republican Party in Arkansas had been on life support since Reconstruction. In the aftermath of the carpetbaggers, Republicans had been branded as the elite, button-down, wealthy few, and the Democrats as the party of the working man. But in the last few decades the Democrats had become the party of pro-abortionists, gay rights supporters, and others who ignore the bedrock tenets of biblical integrity and long-cherished American traditions. Many Arkansas Democrats weren't comfortable with the new regime.

I also knew that becoming a Republican Party candidate would mean facing unjust opposition and burning some bridges.

Anger, Anger Everywhere

When you're a pastor, you make a few people angry, but most of them keep it to themselves. A few bold ones might express their anger at Sunday dinner or in an anonymous letter.

But even those who are really angry with you don't write about it in the newspaper or talk about it on TV.

As soon as I announced I was running for the Senate, however, I was fair game. A candidate becomes something less than a person in that anybody can say anything they want to about you. You soon learn that you're a public figure and you can't defend everything, so you just have to live with it.

Another blow was delivered by the church I served. When I announced my intention to run for office, the church quickly decided to call for a vote on extending my health insurance for the rest of the calendar year—a generous offer. I was preaching somewhere else the night the issue came up for a vote, but unfortunately my children were present. To this day they remember vividly what happened. Church members whom we counted as friends—the very people who had asked me to preach at their husband's funeral or whom I had visited in the hospital, those I had comforted through illness, whom I had counseled through crisis—stood up as if I were a total stranger and said, "Well, I don't think we owe him a dime. If he wants to go off and be a Republican, that's his business. It is none of our concern to worry about his health insurance. Nobody is paying for mine."

Many years of friendship and fellowship were damaged in a single night. People we had poured our hearts into in ministry—families coping with the death of a parent or struggling with drug-addicted children—openly campaigned for my opponent, solely because he was a Democrat. After you have been through the most intense, intimate crisis with someone, you'd think there would be some kind of bond deeper than affiliation with a certain political party. Yet there wasn't. It was hard for us to accept.

We had to work through a lot of things; that was part of our character building. I try to help my children understand that when people say or write ugly things about you, you're going to have a reaction. But don't let it stay with you because then you will become like they are, and we can't afford that. The experience helped them understand that whenever you take a stance, you pay a price for it.

Counting the Cost

At that time my income came from freelance communications work, motivational talks, and speaking in churches. I lost track of the number of times I was scheduled to preach in a Southern Baptist church that year and then got a call from the pastor the week I was supposed to come. He'd say the deacons had met and decided that if I came to speak, they were going to fire the pastor for having a Republican in the pulpit. It was just that plain. It wasn't that I was a *politician*; it was that I was a *Republican*.

Now remember, I had been well accepted as president of our state Baptist convention. I had spoken in most of these churches before and had always been welcome. But suddenly, I became tainted merchandise. It was an extremely painful time, and was especially hurtful to my family. My wife and I both had trouble accepting that people who we thought were our friends never spoke to us again.

Christians often complain about corruption in government and declining morals. You'd think they would have been pleased to have one of their own running for the Senate. But instead of thinking, *We're sending a missionary*, they thought, *we've lost a soul.*

I didn't understand such reasoning. I still don't. People said things like, "Politics is dirty. Christians shouldn't get involved in it." To which I responded, "Everybody wants to eat from a clean plate, but somebody has to do the dishes." It's pointless to gripe about how bad the government is and how terrible the laws are if people who have better ideas are not willing to share them and get involved.

Many Arkansans would have been pleased with what I was doing had I done it as a Democrat. People asked me how many of the Baptists were active in my campaign, and I'd say, "All of them. Half for me and half against." I've never felt such extraordinary hostility and sheer anger. People literally got in my face and yelled.

We were campaigning in Malvern one day, and a woman came up to me and said, "I can't vote for you."

"I understand that you *won't*, but you *can't?*" I replied. "You aren't a convicted felon, are you?"

"No, I'm not."

"Are you not registered in Arkansas?"

"No, I'm a registered voter."

"Well, why can't you vote for me?"

"I'm a Democrat, and I'm a Southern Baptist."

I could tell by this woman's attitude that I had nothing to lose, so I said, "Really? I've always wanted to meet someone who is a Southern Baptist like me but who thinks that taking the life of an unborn child is okay."

"Well, I don't believe that."

I said, "Your party does. I also find it curious that we should share the same spiritual roots but that you would believe that men marrying men would be acceptable."

She said, "I don't believe that."

I said, "Your party is advocating that." I mentioned a couple of other issues that were in the Democratic platform in 1992. The news frustrated her, and she finally barked, "Well, I just want you to know that I'm a Democrat," and stalked off. In other words, don't confuse politics with integrity.

I also got hate mail from total strangers. Typically, they would start out, "I am a Southern Baptist, but . . ." and then, boy, saddle up and get ready for a bumpy ride:

"If you were listening to God, you wouldn't be getting into politics. You've abandoned your call!"

"How can you call yourself a Christian when you don't even realize that you are lowering yourself to a position below your calling?"

"You're *not* called of God. If you were, you wouldn't be a *Republican!*"

From Pulpit to Politics

Yet contrary to the opinion of some, I do not believe there is a huge chasm between careers in church and politics. In fact, I would say there is no better preparation for public office than the pastoral ministry. Pastors and politicians have a lot more in common than a closet full of dark suits. They must master the same four skills to succeed:

1. The ability to communicate a message effectively. You must be able to articulate your feelings, plans, goals, and mandates clearly to your audience. If you can't communicate, it doesn't matter how worthy your ideas are. They'll die on the vine. Nobody will embrace an idea he can't understand.

2. The ability to motivate volunteers. If you can't motivate volunteers, you can't lead a church and you can't run a campaign. Both depend on the enthusiasm and dedication of hundreds or thousands of people who can walk away at any minute. Your only power over them is whatever power they're willing to give you, and they can take it back whenever they want.

3. A clear understanding of the media. You must know how the media works, how to use it effectively, how to harness its influence for your benefit. Whether it's a lectern at the Kiwanis Club or the set of a network television show, you have to be relaxed, confident, and secure. Without this, communication is impossible. So many good people fail here because they insist they "shouldn't have to be a star" to make their point. Maybe they shouldn't, but that's what our society demands of its public figures, whether it's in church or on CNN.

4. The ability to raise money. Churches and political campaigns are both built with voluntary contributions. If you can't raise money, you can't lead a church any more than you can win public office.

Beyond these four key skills, other elements are much the same for both pastors and politicians.

First, you'll never please everybody in either role. You have to deal with issues and make decisions based on information you can't share with anyone, because to do so would violate a confidence. And often, while the decision and implementation might be simple, the thinking behind that decision is anything but simple. You have to make decisions knowing they will be misunderstood, questioned, and often maligned by people who don't know all the facts.

Second, as an officeholder, you're responsible for spending public funds wisely when taxpayers will probably never know if you're wasting their money. As a pastor, I knew there were widows in our church who were tithing on their Social Security checks. Whenever I spent money from the church budget, I needed to think I could look those women in the eyes and say, "I think we spent that money wisely. We have taken good care of what you have entrusted to us." It's the same thing in politics. A public official does not spend his own money. In the church we raise funds through voluntary contributions, while the government gets its money through taxation. Yet in neither case is the money mine. Could I look the citizens of Arkansas in the eyes and say, "We've been responsible with what we took from you. We needed that money and spent it wisely in your best interest"? Good stewardship is very much a part of both politics and the pastorate.

Third, both pastors and politicians must have the ability to persuade people to adopt their point of view. Pastoral and political power are both based on volunteers and voluntary contributions. You can't hold a hammer over your people's heads. Church councils and legislative councils both have to inspire their constituents to follow the direction they set.

Last, families of ministers and those of elected officials are held to different standards than everybody else. I've lived most of my adult life in a fishbowl. Right or wrong, Janet, John Mark, David, and Sarah are put under a public microscope and scrutinized every day. There is a sense in which we're never "off." People expect us to play a certain role once we leave our private quarters. We have to be comfortable with being who we are and must beware of building up some kind of false "public" personality. I think there is a difference between role-playing and role-living. Role-playing is a sham; role-living is being comfortable with who you are anytime an observer walks up to the fishbowl for a look.

And they *will* look—especially when the fishbowl features a few Republicans swimming in a largely Democratic state, but even more so when those Republican "fish" claim ultimate allegiance not to a party, but to the living God.

Let me be clear. The Republican Party is not "God's party" either. God doesn't join our organizations; He asks us to join his. Political parties are simply vehicles to help us get to the place of changing public policy, and some vehicles drive better than others because of their features.

5
YELLOW DOGS BITE

Republican candidates have a tough time campaigning in Arkansas. During the 1992 race, I often had the worst seat at banquets and fish fries and was pointedly ignored by event organizers. In parades, my car was put at the end of the line behind the horses, along with the street sweeper and the fire truck. They would literally hold my car back as the other candidates pulled into position, then send me in last. They didn't even try to be subtle about it.

The Clinton presidential race dominated media coverage that year. His national campaign headquarters was in Little Rock, which meant reporters from around the world were camped out there to cover the campaign. It was the first time an Arkansan had ever been a major party nominee for president, and voter turnout in the state was off the charts. The downside was that every day, news about the Senate race was at the bottom of the front page or halfway through a TV newscast. We just couldn't make enough noise.

The bad news was that we lost the race. The good news was that we got 40 percent of the vote even though we were heavily outspent and even though an Arkansas Democrat was elected president. George Bush's approval rating just after Desert Storm had been 91 percent, and he lost the White House. Compared with that, 40 percent didn't look so terrible.

Even in defeat, we got credit for running a credible race that left the door open for future opportunities. It showed that I had an army of true-blue supporters. Dick Morris, who became my pollster, said he had never polled anyone whose supporters were so fanatically loyal. "Your voters would swim the Mississippi at flood stage to get to the ballot box on election day," he told me. They would never believe something bad in the news or opinion pages about me, because they knew what I stood for, and they stood for the same things.

When Bill Clinton was elected president, his lieutenant governor, Jim Guy Tucker, became governor under the terms of the state constitution. Then there had to be a special election for lieutenant governor. Since we already had a dedicated, loyal staff that had proved itself in the Senate race, we decided I should enter the field. The combination of my service at the Baptist Convention and the Senate campaign had given me a higher profile than any Republican had enjoyed in years. Still, it was an uphill battle.

There is a particular kind of voter in the South called a yellow dog Democrat—a person who will vote Democratic even if the candidate is a yellow dog. Though many people agreed with my positions on the issues, my party label was more than they could stand. There were newspapers in the state that not only wouldn't cover me as a candidate but would forbid the editor to come out and shake my hand. I'd ride in local parades and well-dressed, middle-aged women would make obscene gestures and yell, "We don't like you and we don't want you here! We're not voting for you!"

Several factors contributed to my victory in the lieutenant governor's race in July 1993. First, our team had just been through the Senate race and had learned so much from the experience. Second, we had a clear, consistent message of honesty and integrity that resonated with voters. Third, we took our opponents by surprise. They had campaigned against weak opposition for so long that they weren't prepared to take us on.

Yet even as lieutenant governor, I had those yellow dogs on my tail all the time. Wayne Hogan, a friend in the office supply business, loaned me a desk for the lieutenant governor's office because, once I got the door un-nailed, there was no furniture inside and I couldn't get any. I often got on an elevator at the capitol and people got out; they refused to ride with me.

During my first year in office, I went to a big summer festival in south Arkansas that politicians always attend. When I got there, they told me to "just sit anyplace you can find." The only place left was in the back of the room. All other elected officials were up on stage to be introduced, including the state senator who was planning to challenge me when I ran for re-election in 1994. So they introduced the various guests, including this state senator, whom they called "our next lieutenant governor." After they had introduced everybody (down to the quorum court members) they said, "We do have some other members here in our audience, including a Republican, Mike Hucka-bee." *A Republican.* They didn't even mention that I was the sitting lieutenant governor.

Those sorts of incidents actually helped me get reelected in 1994. The Democrats unintentionally transformed me from a vile Republican to a friend of the common folk. People in Arkansas really do have a genuine sense of fairness and propri-ety. They may be yellow dog Democrats, but deep down there were a lot of people who seemed to say, "I didn't vote for him, I don't like Republicans, but he won the election—so let's treat him right." They were embarrassed for their own party at the kind of treatment I was receiving, and the sympathy worked in our favor.

The Tucker-Clinton Rivalry

Jim Guy Tucker and I were nothing alike, but initially I had a very good working relationship with him. In fact, I had a much better working relationship with Tucker than he had experienced with Governor Clinton. The two of them had been rivals for years. I knew a person didn't understand Arkansas politics when I heard him talking about how Tucker and Clinton were tied together in a Whitewater conspiracy. Bill Clinton and Jim Guy Tucker mistrusted each other far too much to be partners in any sort of business deal. Privately, neither would say a nice thing about the other. They barely spoke, much less worked together.

Their rivalry went back to 1978, when Clinton was the attorney general running for governor, and Tucker was a congressman running for the Senate. They toyed with the idea of running against each other for either senator or governor and kind of danced around the ring, shadow boxing. Clinton ran for governor and won; Tucker ran for the Senate and lost. In 1982, when Clinton was making his comeback after having been voted out of office in 1980, Tucker ran against him in the Democratic primary. Clinton beat Tucker, and the bitterness between them intensified.

Tucker returned to the private sector and nearly disappeared until announcing he would run for governor again in 1990. He made that decision because Clinton hinted he wasn't going to run for re-election. Taking the cue, Tucker announced his candidacy and spent $100,000 getting the ball rolling.

Then Clinton called a press conference in the rotunda of the state capitol. Dick Morris told me later that the purpose of the event was for Clinton to announce publicly he wasn't going to run for re-election. That was the news everybody was expecting and it was what Clinton planned to say. But as he spoke to his supporters, he could not bring himself to declare he wasn't running. Not even Hillary realized what was going to happen. In the middle of his speech, he went from setting up the announcement that he wasn't going to run to saying, "I'm going to run one more time."

Tucker was devastated. He knew he couldn't beat Clinton, so he backed out of the governor's race to run for lieutenant governor, a position in Arkansas that is about as attractive to career politicians as the spit collector in a boxing ring. The lieutenant governor presides over some meetings and has some ceremonial functions, but as far as Tucker was concerned, it was just a perfunctory position. It was a real step down for him.

I've heard people say they suspect Clinton and Tucker made some sort of deal: "Back off and let me get re-elected, then you can move up when I become president." They would never have trusted each other enough for that.

When Clinton became president, Tucker was thrust into the governor's office; but even before that, during the 1992 presidential campaign, Tucker was the *de facto* governor because Clinton was never there. Clinton was not terribly interested in staying governor after 1990. He was running for president the whole time.

What really bothered Tucker was that Clinton would hand unfinished business to him but would never give him the inside information he needed in order to handle it well. It was a tough time. Increasingly, as Clinton got into the presidential campaign, Tucker had more day-to-day impact on managing the government.

When Clinton moved to the White House after the 1992 election, Tucker was furious with him. Clinton left the state in a financial mess, which Tucker had to clean up. Tucker took office on Saturday, December 12, 1992, and called a special session on Monday, December 14, to deal with a state Medicaid funding shortage.

Tucker's Tactics

During Tucker's first months as governor, he and I had a good working relationship. I went out of my way to support things I thought were good. I tried not to be too partisan, and I think he genuinely appreciated my efforts. It was lonely being a Republican in the capitol, but we got along all right.

Things went sour in 1995 amidst increasing talk that Tucker was going to be indicted by the Whitewater grand jury. The special prosecutor was really squeezing him. When the indictment came down in June of 1995, I was careful not to say anything negative. In fact, I was supportive of him; he was innocent until proven guilty. And he was still the state's chief executive.

With all the controversy and talk of felony charges, Governor Tucker knew early in the year he needed to do something to give him the appearance of a strong, visionary, well-respected leader. To do that he pushed three major issues in 1995. Unfortunately, they were three poorly conceived pieces of legislation. The year became a bloodbath that resulted in exactly the opposite impression Tucker was hoping for.

His three big programs were (1) a total change of the public school funding system; (2) a highway construction program; and (3) a rewrite of the state constitution. All three were unpopular with the public.

Tucker's ill-received education plan involved consolidating the state's 311 school districts into thirty-five super districts. When he tried to address a big crowd in Cabot on the issue, they almost booed him off the rostrum. I support local school districts, thinking, *If people are happy with it, who are we to try and tell them they can't have their own school?* The governor's thought was, *These country schools need to be brought into districts with the big city ones, even though country schools are more efficient.*

His highway bill was the worst mess I'd ever seen. It called for the biggest tax increase in state history and huge bonded indebtedness, but he insisted that the legislature vote to hold a public referendum on it. He finally squeezed enough votes to hold the referendum, where he played Santa to the senators, bringing them in one at a time and asking, "And what do you want in your district?"

"Well, I've got to have a new gym for my college."

"I need to have your vote on the highway bill."

"Okay."

These senators would go back to their seats and call out, "I'll vote for it." And when they got the eighteenth person in the thirty-five-member Senate to agree, they called for the vote and passed it. I could hardly believe the number of people who told me to my face that this was the worst piece of legislation they had ever seen, but they voted for it anyway. Holding a public referendum cost the state a million dollars.

The governor's plan for a constitutional convention was originally an inclusive process. He had asked me, along with other Republicans, to work with him so we could examine all sides of the issues freely and openly. Then one night I'd been invited to speak at a Methodist church in Jonesboro. Tucker reached me by cell phone and essentially told me that everything I had been promised was off. There was no way the Democrats were going to let me have any significant role in the constitutional convention, although that statement violated everything we had agreed upon.

What had happened? The governor had caved in to political pressure.

By this time, I had announced that I was going to run for Senate in 1996. The Democrats didn't want to do anything to make me look good, whether it was advising the governor on education reform or being part of a constitutional convention. "This is not what we agreed," I told the governor. "I think you're going to need broad support to make changes in the constitution."

"I don't need your support," he replied. It would be his way or no way. There was no negotiation, no discussion.

I said, "Do what you want, but I can't support you. I have no confidence in this."

In 1996, Arkansas would have an open seat in the U.S. Senate for the first time in eighteen years, and I was ready to go for it. Even though the Whitewater investigation was underway, I didn't think Tucker was guilty and never thought he would be indicted. If he were to go to trial and be convicted, I assumed appeals would drag on for years. By the time it would positively affect the lieutenant governor's position, I thought, I would be long gone to Washington.

In December 1995, the referendum on the constitutional convention failed 80 percent to 20 percent—one of the worst, most lopsided defeats in state history. Tucker put his credibility on the line and got hammered. That made him angry. He blamed me in part for the failure because I had opposed him.

The highway vote was next, scheduled for the following month. I opposed it because of its cost and because it contained so many critical flaws. Not only that, but the Republican Party spent about $200,000 for me to oppose it on TV. Of course, Tucker went ballistic. He was trying to promote this highway program while a TV spot for the opposition featured me as its spokesman. Yet I never attacked him personally; I opposed the highway program exclusively.

The highway referendum lost 87 percent to 13 percent, an even worse defeat than the constitutional convention. The political cartoonists had a field day portraying Tucker as a "lame duck." He wanted to go into his trial looking like a strong, visionary leader who had the support of the people of Arkansas. Instead, he went into that trial having been whipped worse than almost any governor in history in two special elections.

At any time Tucker could have compromised, if only he had realized how out of touch he was and how strongly the people opposed his plans. I think he also got bad advice; his chief adviser was a close friend who was as out of touch with reality as Tucker. Even worse, Tucker had developed a dangerously inflated opinion of his political judgment. He had gotten so focused on the idea of going into his trial with a shining legacy that he developed tunnel vision. He'd lose, but he wouldn't quit. He was absolutely immovable. He would not compromise.

Then when his legislative efforts were defeated, rather than accept responsibility for what happened, he blamed me— particularly for the highway bill. After the defeat of the highway referendum, I saw him only twice for photo-opportunity meetings during the rest of my tenure as lieutenant governor. Aside from those two brief meetings, the next time I heard his voice was on July 15, telling me he had decided not to resign.

Leaders have the responsibility to think and act in the context of their positions. Having been awarded their offices by voters, elected officials in particular must consider the effect their actions will have on others. In trying to pursue his interests rather than the interests of his constituents, Governor Tucker found that his own people had turned against him. Even yellow dog Democrats had had enough.

6
THE CULTURE OF THE MOMENT

Thinking back to that special election for lieutenant governor on July 29, 1993, I can still remember Dick Morris sitting on the edge of his bed in the small, crowded room on the sixth floor of the Camelot Hotel in downtown Little Rock. It was 8:30 p.m., and the polls had been closed for less than an hour. The special election for the office of lieutenant governor was the only item on the ballot in Arkansas that day.

Ordinarily, an election for lieutenant governor would draw little media attention. But this race was different, of course, since the reason for the vacancy was Bill Clinton's move to the White House and Jim Guy Tucker's rise into the governor's seat.

Up to that point in 1993, Republicans across the country had put together a clean sweep of major elections. Later that year, governor's races in New Jersey and Virginia would be claimed by the GOP. But on this sultry day, political eyes nationwide were focused on Arkansas to see what would happen in the new president's backyard.

Morris was no stranger to Arkansas political races or to conducting political polls to determine how those races were going. He had worked for Clinton in every one of the president's political races except his unsuccessful 1974 race for Congress and his unsuccessful 1980 race for governor.

Only a handful of results came in during the first hour after the polls closed at 7:30 p.m. As each new total was posted, Morris would scratch furiously on a yellow legal pad and then enter the figures into a pocket calculator. Just past 8:30 p.m. with less than 15 percent of the precincts having reported, Morris turned to me and in a matter-of-fact tone of voice said, "Congratulations, you're going to be elected lieutenant governor with 51 percent of the vote."

It would be another ninety minutes before the rest of the ballots were counted and the results were clear enough for my opponent to concede and for me to walk on the stage and face a cheering crowd of supporters. Sure enough, I declared victory with 51 percent of the vote. How could he possibly have known the outcome so much earlier, and with so little information?

Where the Polls Stop Counting

That night, I began understanding the power of scientific polling to recognize trends, attitudes, and movement of public opinion. In today's politics, having a competent pollster can be expensive, but not nearly as expensive as not having the information the pollster can generate. Good information ensures that the right campaign decisions are made.

During subsequent campaigns, I have come to appreciate even more the value of public opinion research. It helps make sure the campaign message is having the desired impact on the voters.

Polling is much like using a thermometer, which can read the temperature and give an accurate assessment of where things stand at a given moment. What polling cannot do, however, is serve as a thermostat capable of not only reading the temperature but adjusting it and making it what it should be.

It is important for a political candidate to know what the public believes. But for a candidate to express a belief only because it reflects public sentiment is not what a republican form of government is about. A pressing need of our culture is people whose lives are built upon clear, carefully considered principles. Too many people are being led by those who make decisions based only on what people claim to want rather than what is right or wrong.

As a teenager in my hometown of Hope, Arkansas, I often would hear my pastor say, "If you don't stand for something, you will fall for anything." Corporate leaders, political leaders, church leaders, and families are at their best when they are motivated by principles rather than by public opinion.

The Perfect Ten

What are some principles worth living by? Ask a roomful of people, and you possibly will get a roomful of answers. But there already exists a code of principles established thousands of years ago and adhered to by people from a variety of religious backgrounds. It has been accepted as a basis for appropriate behavior. Fortunately, no one has copyrighted the Ten Commandments.

Although some attempts have been made to prohibit these principles from being displayed, they have survived through the ages. They are the foundation for most of our laws and commonly accepted codes of human behavior.

Law always reveals the character of the people who created it. Therefore, God's law reveals the character of a God who delivered it. In the Ten Commandments, law is the track on which the train of love rides. Law is the imperative of love. The essence of the Ten Commandments is to depict what love looks like.

The Ten Commandments are divided into two sections—the vertical laws dealing with man's relationship with God and the horizontal laws dealing with man's relationship with others. Jesus would say the entire law could be summed up in two basic principles: To love God with all of your heart and to love your neighbor as yourself. This essentially captures our responsibility to God and to others.

Some people have attempted to portray the "thou shalt not" of the law to be essentially negative. Understood in the proper context, however, these commandments are positive affirmations of life-giving, legacy-building principles. Here is a look at the basic laws that appear in Exodus 20:1–17:

1. *You shall have no other gods before me.* This is an affirmation that God can be known in such a way as to create a relationship strong enough to dismiss the need for further searching.

2. *You shall not make for yourself an idol.* The Creator God cannot be confined to a tangible object that can be sold, lost, or destroyed. A god who is visible is a god who is definable and therefore limited to the form in which it exists. The true God cannot be confined. He refuses to conform to our culture.

3. *You shall not misuse the name of the Lord your God.* This principle affirms that God's name should not be used carelessly. One must not treat his love with contempt.

4. *Remember the Sabbath day by keeping it holy.* True love makes special time for those who are loved. The principle behind a day of rest was not to have a day when we forget God but a day when we remember him.

5. *Honor your father and your mother.* Real love respects authority. A person must learn to cope with authority first in the home.

6. *You shall not murder.* This commandment is an affirmation of the sacredness of human life and a reminder that the real goal of love is always to heal, not to hurt.

7. *You shall not commit adultery.* The devastation of adultery is that it defrauds the love of another and destroys the self-esteem of the one being defrauded. Promises and vows are sacred, and the seventh commandment affirms the validity and authority of such promises.

8. *You shall not steal.* True love has the desire to give instead of take.

9. *You shall not give false testimony against your neighbor.* Gossip and outright falsehoods defy the character of a God who is always honest. Love is always honest. Dr. Vester Wobler was, for many years, chairman of the department of religion at my alma mater, Ouachita Baptist University in Arkadelphia, Arkansas. I still recall his wise advice to his freshmen students. He admonished us to tell the truth and nothing but the truth, but never to be so dumb that we told all the truth we knew. Some seek to justify the spreading of stories and rumors in the name

of concern or even correction. But each of us should be careful to speak well of others.

10. *You shall not covet.* Love delights in the possessions of others rather than desiring what others have and feeling jealous about what they have.

The law reveals God's depth of character, and it also reveals our lack of character. Laws are a giant mirror reflecting not only what is but projecting what ought to be, giving us the standard against which to compare our lives.

A person who has no standard to live by other than the culture of the moment is a person whose principles might as well come from the latest public opinion polls. This would be like repairing an appliance by holding it against a mirror rather than reading the directions to determine how it should be performing.

7
UNDER THE INFLUENCE

Each of us is the product of many influences—some major, some less important. It's like making stew. There may be more potatoes than tomatoes, but every ingredient makes a difference. When it is all finished, a unique flavor results.

Many people have been key ingredients in my life. The first ones were my parents, working-class people who struggled to make ends meet but who were grateful for what they had and made the most of it. They represented about as pure an America as there is. They had a better life than their parents, but they wanted a better life for their children. They worked hard and carefully instilled a solid work ethic in my sister and me, insisting that no one was going to hand us anything. If we wanted something, we knew we were going to have to work for it.

Teaching by Example

Then there were my teachers. I was fortunate to have an outstanding public education. My teachers in Hope were good people and dedicated instructors. They instilled in me a desire to learn. They introduced us to the biographies of great people, books that had a major influence on me. I read every biography I could find from the second grade on. (Sad to say, many of the biographies written today dwell on the scandalous and irresponsible episodes in a person's life rather than on the accomplishments that earned a person fame. There was no way we ever would have been exposed to the sexual indiscretions of Dwight Eisenhower. He was a great general and a fine president—a positive influence on our culture.)

In high school, teachers had even more of an impact on me. One I particularly remember was Alex Strawn, the speech, drama, and debate coach. He was a young teacher—it was his first assignment—and bursting with idealism, eager to inspire young minds. We were impressionable kids just waiting for someone like him to come along. It was a wonderful combination. He developed a debate program that challenged every brain cell. He pushed us in just the right way to be our best.

Another memorable teacher was Anna E. Williams, the student council adviser. She took me under her wing. From the ninth grade, when I was a student council representative, to twelfth grade, when I was council president, she kept pushing me to do better and to get more done. Mrs. Williams was determined to develop leadership skills in me. She made me visit her for half an hour every morning before school. I'd have to go through my goals for that day and give account for my goals from the day before. She was a list maker and turned me into one.

Today I am a fanatic list maker. And it works. I can tell how good a day I've had by how many things I can check off. This practice of making lists instilled in me a sense of establishing priorities and tracking progress. Mrs. Williams pushed me. No matter how much I accomplished, she would always point out what more I could have done with a little more effort. I look back now and realize she was instilling in me disciplines useful throughout life.

Attending Ouachita Baptist University was an outstanding experience for me. It allowed me to take on the challenge of being with some of the sharpest high school graduates in the state. And the peer pressure was wonderful. What a difference between typical secular college peer pressure and the pressure at Ouachita! While the pressure at a secular school might have been to skip class or guzzle a six-pack with the guys, the pressure at Ouachita was to excel.

So many students competed for academic awards that the party animals usually didn't last more than a semester or two. Those who stayed were serious when it came to their education. Some of them were pranksters, but they didn't go there just to waste four years of their lives. The positive influence of my fellow students was, in part, what helped me get through a four-year program in a little more than two years.

At fourteen I held my first job—working at the radio station in Hope. Haskell Jones, the station manager, was a powerful influence in my life. First, he gave me an opportunity to work. Second, he was very patriotic. If "The Star-Spangled Banner" played on the radio, he would stand up and put his hand over his heart. He instilled in everybody who knew him the idea that the American dream was something to be cherished. He was also one of the few Republicans I knew in Hope. He was true to his beliefs; he didn't care that everyone thought he was a little loony for being a Republican. He was one, and that was the way it was.

Mr. Jones was probably the most community-minded person I have ever known. Whenever there was a need, we would do radiothons. If there was some little girl who was desperately ill and needed a transplant or special treatment, Mr. Jones would see to it. That was before health insurance became so prevalent, and those were proud southern people. If somebody was in need, we'd spend a whole Saturday on the radio raising money. I just assumed everybody thought you should give something back to your community—through the chamber of commerce, United Way, or a civic club. I've tried to follow his example; I've always been involved in community organizations and projects.

As I look back, it's hard to imagine someone who would turn a radio station over to a fourteen-year-old kid. I would be there all by myself. I'd turn the transmitter on in the morning, do the news and the weather, and play records. At our church's television station in Texarkana, I wouldn't let a fourteen-year-old answer the phone, much less run the whole station!

Growing Up in Church

I grew up in a small Missionary Baptist church, and at the time the theology that dominated those churches in the South was somewhat legalistic. Although today I believe this emphasis is misguided, it probably protected me from dangerous experiments that damaged peers.

The other side of the coin was that there was a heavy emphasis on Scripture, Bible study, and memorization—all of which will serve me for the rest of my life. My pastors and Sunday school teachers had a big influence on me. Some were particularly helpful in getting me to see the value of Scripture. I was inquisitive and liked to ask questions about "why can't we?" or "why is it wrong?" I was not satisfied when the answers were, "You're just not supposed to."

"Well, why? Why is that wrong?"

"Because . . . it's just not the way we're supposed to do it."

When I was fourteen or fifteen, I went through a period of disenchantment with such non-answers. I know it's tempting to say, "Because the Bible says it's wrong," and leave it at that. But there are reasons *why* the Bible says it's wrong, and there are rational, appropriate foundations for the prohibitions we find in God's Word. Part of my rebellion was toward this can't-do mentality. I wanted to know what I *could* do. Tell me something that is positive, tell me something that is worthy of my life, something I can invest myself in. Don't just give me a list of restrictions!

My own experience has taught me that we can't get by with telling teenagers, "Just because!" when it comes to spiritual matters. We need to give them the principles behind the rules. They may not agree with them, but at least we have given them a basis to understand the "why" when we tell them not to drink or whatever.

My early struggle with legalism greatly affected my walk with the Lord. Today I am definitely a "grace Christian" and not a "law Christian." One of the few things I detest more than liberalism is legalism. I think both are cancers to the Christian faith—liberalism because it doesn't believe anything, and legalism because it restricts us only to the things we can live up to. Liberalism makes God seem so commonplace that He becomes meaningless, while legalism makes God so small that He becomes insignificant.

The negative aspect of a legalistic worldview is that you create what becomes your own Christian faith. It's really a set of do's and don'ts that allow someone to judge whether others are good people or good Christians. The problem is, we're always going to create a list we can live up to, which means we're not living up to the standards of Jesus Christ. We are merely living up to the standards of our list, which is a form of self-idolatry. "Don't smoke, don't drink, pet your dog every day—if you can do all those things, then you redeem yourself," even though your life may be filled with jealousy, greed, lust, and every other deadly vice.

Dealing with situations as a pastor, I became keenly aware of our utter failure as human beings to live up to the pure standard of God. Even the best people I knew fell hopelessly short, which convinced me even more of the need for grace. I came to understand the importance of the cross, the divine bridge between God and man. I grew up with *The Four Spiritual Laws* and knew about the big gap between us and God—but hearing that and seeing it in people's lives are two different things. Fortunately, God is gracious. And just as He exercises grace toward me, I have to exercise grace toward others. It's easy to want Him to exercise grace toward me; the real reach is becoming anxious for Him to exercise grace toward others.

Today, grace affects everything I think and do. In every decision I make as a governor, as a father, a spouse, or a friend, it has an impact on me. When I think of Anna Williams, Haskell Jones, and other important people in my life, I remember both their inspiring encouragement and their eagerness to see me succeed. God gave them to me as examples of how we can grant grace to each other. I pray I never lose sight of the lessons they taught.

8
JANET

I have heard that people often marry their opposites. It's certainly true in my marriage. I like to engage in thoughtful discourse on why we are doing something, trying to clarify our goals; Janet just wants to get it done. I will take nonphysical risks, such as running for office or taking a job that may not work out; Janet will take physical risks—climbing cliffs, parasailing, racing cars, or stalking bears.

Janet's sense of adventure attracted me when we were both high school students in Hope. Another attraction was her spiritual strength. People can provide some of the moral anchors we need in life, and my most extraordinary anchor is Janet.

My wife's physical stamina and moral strength were shaped by challenges she faced early in life. Her father left her family (Janet, her mother, two brothers, and two sisters) when she was a child. Her mother had no choice but to tough it out. They had to stretch a single, modest paycheck to cover all six of them.

Janet grew up learning to be frugal, to share, and to develop a lot of independence. In her life, the mother was the primary role model, so she had quite a different perspective of family responsibilities than I had. Even today, if something needs to be fixed, she fixes it.

I am utterly inept when it comes to mechanical things. My father, on the other hand, was a talented mechanic. He liked physical labor. He did everything from wiring houses to putting out fires, and on his days off he was a mechanic in his little generator shop. If something needed to be done around the house, he would do it. He could fix things much better than he could explain to a child how to do it. Rather than, "Let me show you how," he'd say, "Just let me get this done." Consequently, I appreciate the fact that Janet can change tires.

Another episode in her life also helps to account for her courage and strength. During the first year of our marriage, she was diagnosed with cancer of the spine. That was a traumatic time in our lives, but her resolve carried her through. Despite the doctors' dire predictions, she completely recovered.

Janet's faith and stamina were tested again three years after John Mark was born. She became pregnant again but miscarried after about three months. Rather than letting the tragedy of that loss consume her, she came out of it even stronger. Her faith was unshaken.

She ended up learning and growing through all of it. Otherwise, I'm not sure how she would have reacted to a husband who went from communications to the pastorate to politics.

Tender Heart but Tough As Nails

Janet is also fearless and has a tough exterior to protect the inside, which is, frankly, vulnerable. Don't get me wrong. She's not tough in the sense of cruel—people love her when they get to know her—but she's tough in that she will stand up for herself and others when she feels someone is being abused or marginalized. She has a sensitive heart for people who are being abused and abhors it when someone looks down his nose at someone else.

For her, one of the most difficult aspects of being Arkansas' first lady was the inevitable confrontation with some of the snobby elitists who had always been on the side of the culturally correct in Little Rock. We're a little more informal, and we make no excuses for it. Janet also had to contend with nitpickers about everything from what she wore to what furniture she moved into the governor's mansion. It just went with the territory, and she handled it with admirable grace.

One of Little Rock's liberal, cynical newspaper columnists wrote a piece about Janet's doings at the mansion, so she called him up and asked, "Have you been to the mansion lately? Why don't you just come over here, and I'll show you what's going on." She spent an hour and a half taking him all over the place, even up in the attic. That's her style. She didn't sit around and brood about it. She called and invited him to see what the real situation was.

If being a wife in the public fishbowl is tough, being a mother is worse. It presented all kinds of challenges for her. I think the best preparation my children could have had for playing the role of "the governor's kids" was being "the preacher's kids." Their whole lives, people expected them to be either perfect or horrible. If they acted up, I heard, "Hey, what do you expect? They're the preacher's kids." Or folks expected them to be perfect and were flabbergasted when they weren't: "I can't believe you would do that when your *father* is a *pastor.*" It's exactly the same when your father is governor. And, of course, Janet felt the full force of these harsh comments when they hit.

Our kids were also used to having their father criticized and critiqued by people who didn't know the facts. Before, it was a barbed comment about a sermon. Now, it's about a speech or policy decision. The situation is intensified, the light is hotter, the audience is bigger, but it's basically the same. The major difference is that in church, although they put you on a pedestal and scrutinize you as you swim around the fishbowl, they really want you to succeed because you are their model. In politics, they also put you on a pedestal, but there they want you to fail. They want to take comfort in knowing you aren't any better than they are.

To overcome some of this oversized scrutiny, Janet and I both did what we could to help our children lead normal lives. For example, our daughter was on a mock trial team in junior high. In the spring of 1997, the team went to the national finals—the first time a junior high team had ever gone from Arkansas. Janet accompanied the team, not as the first lady but as a mother going on a field trip.

Raising the Bar

Janet is also an extremely effective fund-raiser. Don't ask her to help unless you are serious; otherwise, she'll wear you out. When the Florence Crittenton Home, a haven for unwed mothers in Little Rock, asked for her help, she led an effort that eventually surpassed the previous fundraising record by $30,000. She headed fund-raising for the Red Cross after the 1997 tornadoes; they set a goal of $100,000 and raised $165,000. She rode in an American Lung Association bike race, biking sixty-three miles in one day from Little Rock to Hot Springs. She led the Shots for Tots campaign in Arkansas, whose goal was to get the children of the state immunized. The state health director asked her to head the campaign. Their goal was 90 percent compliance until Janet said, "We'd better make it 95 percent." They changed the goal.

Beyond all doubt, Janet is a person of action. Talking policy bores her; she's interested in implementation. Her philosophy on how to accomplish welfare reform sounds like something from John Wayne: "Saddle up, pilgrim, and get to work." She is more the type to get down on the floor and play with the kids than to lecture them on the fine art of government. She likes to be involved in the action far more than to debate the philosophy behind it.

Once, when Janet was chaperoning a group of graduating high school students a couple of years ago, they went to a place that offered bungee jumping. Some of the students saw it and were thinking about giving it a try, but then they backed down. So Janet said, "Well, I'll do it."

And she did. Twice. I've seen the video.

PART II

THE NEED FOR CHARACTER

9
THE MORAL THERMOSTAT

In one of our few brief meetings before I assumed the office of governor, Jim Guy Tucker told me about a cabinet member he was going to fire. The governor said he would do me a favor and fire him before I had to take him. I listened and said, "If that is what you think of his work, it's okay with me. He's a nice guy, but I never have evaluated him. It's your call."

Later I was told Tucker's chief of staff called the man in and said, "We've got to fire you because the lieutenant governor wants us to get rid of you before he takes office."

The man immediately came to me and asked, "Did you order me fired?"

I told him I hadn't. He played a tape of the conversation; I was incredulous. "That is absolutely untrue!" I said. "He told me *he* wanted to fire you." I hired the man to head another department, and he did a splendid job in that position.

As I mentioned in an earlier chapter, I had informed Tucker that I wanted to keep some clerical workers. We wanted at least some people who knew where the bathrooms were. Besides that, we wanted to see how many would like to stay; we didn't want to throw everybody out. Tucker's aides told them, "You are going to lose your jobs. You won't have a job after we leave, so just get ready to go."

We thought employees were being told they could apply to keep their jobs. When we received only three or four résumés out of almost fifty staffers, we knew something wasn't right. Finally a staff member said, "Tucker's chief of staff told us it didn't make any difference what we did, we wouldn't be hired anyway." I was stunned. I asked to meet with the employees and told them that while we couldn't keep policy-level senior staff, we would like some others to stay. They became some of the most fulfilled, dedicated, outstanding public servants in the state.

The Root of Character

Treating people with integrity and respect is the only way to get them to achieve their full potential. And it isn't just a matter of saying character counts and leaving it at that. Character *does* count. Integrity *does* count. But if integrity and character are divorced from God, they don't make sense. If you try to set your own moral thermostat, chances are that a lot of other people will be uncomfortable. Integrity, left to define itself, becomes evil because everyone ends up choosing his own standards.

One afternoon when my son John Mark was twelve, he didn't want to go shopping with the rest of the family so he stayed home. When we returned, he walked up to me, beaming, and said, "Dad, I did something while you were gone. I made a cake!" This was totally out of character for him. He was so excited, and I was so proud that he had done something unselfish for us. Thinking back to seminars that said "encourage your children; give them lots of praise," I got ready to praise this cake.

He said, "Here, I want you to have the first piece."

It looked pretty good, and as I sank my teeth into the first bite, I determined that praise would flow out of my mouth for this wonderfully selfless gift. Unfortunately, only cake flowed out of my mouth as I involuntarily spit it out. That cake was atrocious! *This kid is trying to kill me!* I thought. I asked him, gently, "Did you follow a recipe for this cake?"

"Yes sir," he answered.

"Could I see that recipe?"

"Yes sir."

The recipe looked perfectly acceptable. "Are you sure you followed this recipe exactly?"

"Yes sir, I promise I followed the recipe exactly . . . except for one thing. It said to add a dash of salt. I didn't know what a dash was, but I figured a cup ought to take care of it."

He had put a full cup of salt in his cake. A cow could have licked on it for six months and still had some left.

The point of the story is: my son's motives were honorable and sincere. His efforts were diligent, and he finished the task he had set out to do following the instructions as he understood them. There was only one problem: no one had defined for him what a "dash" was. It was an unknown standard. So he made up his own standard. The results were utterly disastrous.

In the same way, we're afraid in this country today to define for our children what is right and wrong. Instead, we say, "You'll have to find out for yourself," or "Do whatever seems good for you." We tell them, "It doesn't matter what you believe as long as you are sincere," and "Do your best." Such misguided sentiments are the tragic products of our morally relativistic generation. We believe fairness is more important than accuracy, that effort counts for more than excellence, that participation is as good as achievement.

We are scared to death to say, "That's wrong." We want to say, "You have a disorder or a disability," or any of the scores of euphemisms people use. Yet all we're doing is struggling to cover up immoral, improper, illegal, or boorish behavior.

We try to excuse it. "He was just expressing himself. Don't squash his creativity!" But children need to be disciplined and to know there are lines they must live within.

When a pilot flies into a city, he encounters miles of concrete in all directions; but it is crucial that the pilot lands only on a particular strip of concrete to which the air traffic controller has directed him. If he lands on the freeway in rush-hour traffic, hundreds of people could die. Is it narrow-minded to limit him to that one strip of concrete? Perhaps so, but anything else leads to disaster.

Our children must be told which concrete is safe to land on. Too often we fail to say, "*This* is right; anything else is wrong." Instead, we say, "Wherever you want to go is fine." There are a lot of places in Little Rock where there's room to land a jetliner, and most of them are wrong.

We refuse to direct our children and then run around moaning, "What is wrong with our kids today? Look at the violence! Look at the decadence! Look at the drug addiction and alcohol addiction and the lack of respect!" Why are we moaning? *We trained them to be this way.*

There has to be an immovable standard. A solid foundation. A moral thermostat whose setting is not subject to the whim of personal opinion.

On March 1, 1997, a tornado cut a 260-mile path of destruction through Arkansas. We went up to Jacksonport, one of the most devastated communities, to survey the damage. As soon as we got off the helicopter, state representative Martha Shoffner of Newport met me and said, "Governor, I've got to show you something you won't believe." We drove into town and entered a museum in the old courthouse. The tornado had torn off most of the roof, and the interior was trashed by the storm.

Everything in the room was either blown away or ruined, except for one item: a picture of me as governor, hanging on the wall. It was still there; it hadn't moved or even as much as tilted. The thought occurred to me that during all the storms and ferocious pressures that blow into our lives, we must stand firm. You can't stop storms, and you can't hide from them. All you can hope for is that when the storms hit, you are able to stay put.

Live Narrowly, Love Broadly

Being a Christian makes it possible to stay put. But I think many well-meaning Christians mistakenly think that because they recognize the value of integrity, they should avoid people who don't. That is a grave error. Christians who understand their faith are not exclusive, but inclusive.

Jesus was the most inclusive person in the world. He lived life within narrowly defined boundaries, but He loved broadly, reaching out to people from every conceivable walk of life. I'm afraid we too often twist that around; we have a broad life and love narrowly. Many contemporary believers love people only like themselves: white, middle-class church members who practice the same habits and avoid the same behaviors. They don't know many people who are Jewish or black, poor or wealthy. What a tragedy.

Being governor gave me an opportunity to practice my faith with a broad range of people. After the tornado, there were practical things I could do to help people rebuild their communities. But I also had the opportunity to bring some sense of consolation, some sense of perspective to the situation. What a privilege to offer hope in the midst of what looked like an utterly hopeless situation.

It's humbling to kneel down and take the hand of an elderly lady sitting in a borrowed lawn chair, in front of what used to be her house. Her husband of forty-two years had been killed in the storm. In many ways I was more of a pastor than a governor during that time. There were times when I felt I was pastoring a 2.5-million-member church.

Crises like that provide a true test of character. Is there looting, or do neighbors pitch in and help each other? Do victims file accurate claims? Do insurance companies pay promptly? I agree with the writer who said that "character is the person you are when no one is looking." It's the person you are when the cameras are off, the witnesses are gone, and there's no one to keep score.

I think we all are performers to some extent. But the real person is the one who is as nearly the same behind closed doors as in the public eye. We might say, "I'd never steal with someone watching me." But would we steal if no one was watching? We'd never lie if we thought someone might find out; but would we lie if we thought no one would ever know? Those are the real issues of life—not "What can I get by with?" but "What do I want to get by with?"

It seems to me that the desire to see public officials fail the integrity test is at an all-time high. The media is saturated with it. The reason for this, I believe, is that by showing the character flaws in other people, the public affirms that its own inadequacies are really not so abnormal. As the character of America begins to plummet, we want to justify our own lack of morality by somehow showing that everyone is just as bad.

People who lie think everyone is a liar. Thieves think everyone steals. People who are insincere in their comments and actions think everyone else is insincere. Therefore, people who are essentially unethical think everyone is unethical, and they're determined to find it in you. If you're not overtly flawed, you become a contrast and a threat. It's proof of the biblical statement that men are lovers of darkness rather than light, because the light exposes their dark deeds.

I am reminded of when I was a little kid at a church camp in Gary, Texas. There was a 10 p.m. lights-out policy. As soon as the lights were off and the counselor was snoring, the guys would get up, fish out their hidden Cheerios and M&Ms, and start crawling around in the rafters of the barracks. When the counselor heard something and flipped on the lights, everybody would scramble around like cockroaches and jump into the nearest bed. In the dark, we misbehaved; in the light, we hid in fear.

That's what has happened to the public at large. People are desperate to justify their own immoral attitudes by saying, "He's a failure, too, so I'm as good as he is." Our generation has learned to hold to the standard of each other instead of the standard of God. That is the travesty: God is no longer the standard; we are.

10
THE ULTIMATE QUESTION

There's a continuing debate about why American society has renounced its traditional standards of integrity. Many people agree that, as a nation, we once recognized a common standard and that somehow we've drifted away from it. The "right thing" today is subjective, which has caused problems with everything from discipline in the schools to pornography on the Internet.

How did we move in one generation from a society with a shared, confident sense of right to a society of relativism and moral decay?

No Single Answer

The first step to answering that question is to admit there isn't just one answer. I've heard that it all started when we took prayer out of schools. That's a simplistic answer. It wasn't just prayer in schools; it wasn't just television; it wasn't just Watergate; it wasn't just welfare. It wasn't any one thing.

There is a story about an old farmer who was sitting on his porch one day when a salesman came to call. As he stepped onto the porch, the salesman saw a pig in the front yard with only three legs. The fourth leg was wooden.

"Is that really a pig with a wooden leg?" the salesman asked.

"Yeah, it is," the farmer drawled.

"But how come that pig has a wooden leg?" inquired the salesman.

"Well, that's a right smart pig," answered the farmer. "I was down there plowing the field one day, and the tractor fell over and pinned me to the ground. I would have died, but that pig saw what happened and came over and dug me out from under the tractor. He saved my life."

"That's incredible," the astonished salesman replied. "But it doesn't explain why he has a wooden leg."

"You don't seem to understand, mister," continued the farmer. "I said that was a smart pig. One night we were all in the house asleep, and the house caught fire. We didn't even smell the smoke—my wife, my kids and me. That pig started snorting and squealing and making all kinds of noise, and we woke up and realized our house was on fire. The pig saved us and saved our house."

"That's the most amazing story I ever heard," said the salesman. "But you still haven't answered my question. Why does the pig have a wooden leg?"

The farmer replied, "Mister, you don't think that if we had a pig that smart we'd be stupid enough to eat him all at once!"

If any force is going to overcome a free, prosperous country like America, it won't happen all at once. America has a solid foundation of liberty, personal dignity, and opportunity. Anybody can rise above his social circumstances. There's no caste system. You don't have to be a member of the nobility to get ahead.

The only way to destroy something with that kind of foundation is to chip away at it, one value at a time. Take away its heart and essence. Bring doubt to what used to be confidence, denial to what used to be faith, death to what was life. I think that is what has happened.

Contrast the generation of the Great Depression with the generation of today. During the Depression, people were poor, hungry, and out of work. Yet they didn't engage in the kind of gang violence we have in schools today. Students weren't killing each other for a pair of shoes. Crime could easily have been justified by saying, "I'm hungry, and I don't have as much as you; therefore, I have a right to take what I can get." Dishonesty was still considered wrong, and thieves were despised.

Public officials and the policies they set show how far we have drifted, one tiny step at a time. When I was president of the Arkansas Baptist State Convention, Bill Clinton was governor. Clinton was experienced and savvy enough to recognize that the half-million Baptists in the state were probably the largest constituency he had. His antenna was attuned to that constituency, and from time to time he and I would discuss various issues.

During a heated discussion on abortion, Dr. Joycelyn Elders told Christians they needed to "get over their love affair with the fetus"—an infamous phrase that was often repeated after she became surgeon general. The comment outraged even non-Christians. but it particularly offended conservative believers. Governor Clinton called me and wanted to know how much of a problem this kind of comment was causing. I told him it was a serious problem. She had deeply offended many people. It was a slap in the face to those who held pro-life convictions.

"I wish you would explain to her how people in the evangelical world feel," he said. "Would you be willing to talk with her?"

I said I'd be happy to. So he set up a meeting and I went to visit her. We talked in her office for several hours. After we finished, I recognized she was absolutely sincere in her beliefs. I also realized that the reason her positions on these issues so conflicted with mine was that our worldviews were fundamentally at odds. Reaching a consensus was impossible. Like my son and his cake-baking experience, she had her own idea of what a "dash" of salt was—in this case a "dash" of human life—and recognized no fixed standard that could show her she was wrong.

We agreed there were problems with crime, poverty, disease, and other social ills. Where we disagreed was in identifying the source of the problems. She said they came from ignorance. She thought people needed to be educated and that we had a sexually transmitted disease problem because of a lack of education. Her solution therefore was sex education, drug education, and AIDS education in our schools. If we educated people about the risks of those types of behavior, they would avoid them. If we educated them in general knowledge—math, science, English, history—people would do better because they would know better. Then we could eliminate crime. In her view, our problems continued to plague us, essentially because of economics: if we only poured more money into education, education could wipe the slate clean.

Is Man Good?

Dr. Elders argued that man is basically good; therefore, if he does bad things, he simply doesn't realize they are bad, or else he hasn't been trained to do good. Her solution was to tell people, "This is a good way to live. You are really not a bad person; you just haven't found your goodness yet."

It sounds noble and, frankly, it seems a much more appealing approach to life than the alternative. It has but a single flaw: it's wrong. It will never work because our problems do not result from economics or deficiencies in education. They result from the selfish decision to ignore God's standards of integrity. Standards based on anything else are relative, and relative standards are meaningless.

A person with a biblical worldview says humans are by nature selfish. We are not basically good; rather, we are basically self-centered, look out for ourselves first, and preserve ourselves first at all costs. Only two things will change this behavior: either our nature will be changed by a supernatural experience with God through Christ, or we will fear the consequences of not doing the right thing. If we remove those consequences and make it easy to steal and lie with impunity, then we will do those things freely. We will do whatever brings us pleasure.

The biblical book of Judges describes one of the darkest times in Old Testament history, and it uses one unforgettable line to explain the reason for the darkness: "Everyone did what was right in his own eyes" (21:25). That is precisely where we are today.

You hear it in our language. "If it feels good, do it." "What's in it for me?" Advertising slogans underscore the trend. "We do it all for you." "Have it your way." "You deserve a break today." "This Bud's for you." They all appeal to our basic, selfish nature—we are deserving, and we are good.

Those who believe God created humans have a different worldview from those who believe humans created God. Are we here to have nature serve us, or are we here because we are to serve nature? Politics are totally directed by worldview. That's why when people say, "We ought to separate politics from religion," I say to separate the two is absolutely impossible.

When Man Becomes God

Public debate today is filled with arguments that, not long ago, would have been dismissed as ridiculous and insupportable. Consider homosexuality, for instance. There have been homosexuals in every human culture. But until recently, who would have dared to suggest that the practice should be accepted on equal footing with heterosexuality, to be thought of as a personal decision and nothing more?

Abortion also became okay because we decided it is okay. Where did we get the right to make that decision? Because we're our own god. If the inconvenience of that little child would interrupt our college education or a relationship with a boyfriend or girlfriend, then that child becomes nothing more than a choice. "It's my choice. I decide for myself. What about me?" That is the essence of our culture.

Everything you do and believe in is directed by your answer to the ultimate question: Is there a God? It all comes down to that single issue. If there is a God, then everything moves one way. If there isn't, it moves another.

The next question is this: If there is a God, can we know Him? If we can't know Him, then it doesn't matter whether He exists. But if we can know Him, that knowledge fundamentally directs our lives.

Subsequent questions naturally follow from this. If we *can* know Him, then *how* can we know Him? How does He reveal Himself to us? If we can know Him, and if He does reveal Himself, how does He relate to me? What does He expect of me? How am I accountable to Him? What happens if I am not accountable to Him? My whole life will be directed by the value I place on the answers to those questions.

On the other hand, if I believe that I somehow created God because I needed some explanation for the inexplicable; if I believe the only real world is the one I'm living in right now, and that when I die I will turn back to dust and that there isn't any more than that, then I will live only for myself and only for the moment. God might have given me some sort of ability to cope with the perplexities of life. I might use Christian terms and practice some civil religion, but it doesn't substantially change my behavior because I don't really believe I will have to give account of my actions someday.

Everything comes down to the faith question, which then leads to the integrity question: Where does integrity of character come from? Either it comes from God, or it comes from something we manufacture. If it comes from God, it is fixed.

Of course, in practice we will invariably fall short of perfection, but our practice will always butt against a fixed absolute—the standard that is the same yesterday, today, and forever. The standard my grandfather had will be the same standard my grandchildren will have. We may pull away from it further and more often, but the standard stays.

If I don't believe there is a God, then I don't believe character is fixed. I believe it moves as the culture moves. Therefore, what was wrong once is no longer wrong because the culture no longer considers it inappropriate; we are able to move the standards. Proverbs 23:10 warns against moving "the ancient landmark" or boundary stone set by our forefathers. That means that once you move your reference point, everything else becomes chaos.

After the tornado devastated my state in 1997, I was visiting Arkadelphia. I had lived there when I was in college. That was where Janet and I first lived as a couple, so the town was familiar to me. But everything I remembered about the place had vanished. There was so much devastation that when I stood in the middle of town, I could find no familiar reference points. Not a wall, not a sign. Nothing but piles of rubble for blocks and blocks.

Had there been one landmark—say, the hardware store—I could have identified everything else in town, even though it lay in ruins. Across the street, that pile of debris used to be a shoe store. Two blocks down, that twisted steel was a government office. But with no reference points, I was completely lost.

That is essentially what is happening to our society. We're lost because we recognize no fixed reference point. By refusing to define character using fixed standards, we lose our reference point, we lose our ability to navigate, and, therefore, we drift. Who is right and who is wrong? Who knows?

There is obviously a sense of order in the world. If there weren't, we wouldn't be here; there would only be a mass of molecules swirling around in the universe. Instead we have oak trees and rose blossoms and the delicate twists and turns of a newborn baby's ear. That order could only be directed and ordained by God. The same Master who fixed the seasons of the year and put the birds in the sky is the solid, unmoving reference point we must fix our lives on.

Does God exist? He has to, or we wouldn't exist ourselves.

11
FAITH IS LIKE A BASS BOAT

Our faith determines how we react to the culture in which we live. Because it so fundamentally defines us, we can't allow faith to take a secondary role in making day-to-day decisions.

I took a lot of heat as a candidate for "dirtying" my calling as a pastor. No one pretends that politics is pretty or clean. But that's why Christians need to get involved. The less salt and light there is in a place, the more beneficial the Christian point of view can be.

Christians can't refuse to get involved in an issue because it's messy; that's where they're needed most. Jesus didn't avoid the unwashed. He ministered to them. He even ate dinner with a tax collector! Christians need to pull on their hip boots and wade into the swamp of social and moral issues. It's hard to "rescue the perishing" if we're standing on the bank in freshly laundered clothes, refusing to get a little dirty.

I love to fish. Fortunately, fishing was one recreational activity I could still enjoy as governor. By myself or with members of my family, I could occasionally slip off to the Arkansas River for a couple of hours without causing a lot of commotion. (The other leisure activity I could still get away with was going to movies. Once I was inside the theater and it was dark, my presence caused no disruption.)

From time to time, I still fish for trout in some of Arkansas's premier streams, but my favorite is bass fishing. I like the strategy and the challenge. I also enjoy the quiet and the chance to visit in a relaxed environment with Janet, the children, or some good friends. For my fortieth birthday, Janet surprised me with a fabulous bass boat—a metallic blue BassCat Pantera II with casting chairs, a 150-horsepower Mercury outboard, a fish finder, and even a stereo! The boat was parked in back of the governor's mansion so I could see it whenever I looked out of the breakfast room windows.

Sitting there in the sunlight, its metallic paint sparkled, its controls and instruments glistened, and the trailer shined. That rig would be the envy of any true bass angler. But it looked pristine only as long as it was sitting in the driveway. To get any use out of it, I had to be willing to get it dirty.

I can imagine some proud fisherman who spends all day cleaning, waxing, and shining his boat. The ropes are perfectly coiled, the rods and tackle all neatly stored, the chrome without a single fingerprint. He trailers his rig to boat shows to meet other bass fishermen, also with beautiful rigs. They sit around and talk about how their boats perform—how comfortable the seats are, how roomy the bait lockers are, how fast the engines can get them to their favorite, secret spot on the lake.

They might even put out a newsletter with articles about how to maintain the boats and keep them looking sharp, calendars of upcoming events, and point systems for improving their scores in boat show competitions.

But put those beautiful rigs in the water? Never! Imagine dulling that mirror finish, gained only after months of waxing. River water has sticks, leaves, algae, and goodness knows what else in it. There might even be old logs or stumps under the surface. Someone might spill gasoline in the boat. And think of all the muddy footprints! Yucky bait! Smelly, slimy fish flopping around!

These so-called "fishermen" end up with a beautiful boat, designed and built to do a specific job, which is absolutely useless out of the water. Unless they're willing to get it dirty, the boat is of no value.

Use Your Faith

Faith is like a bass boat. If we acquire it just to admire it, we might as well not have it at all. Just feeling self-satisfied with our faith isn't enough. We have to be willing to act on that feeling, to put our faith to the use for which it was meant. We can't stand around bemoaning the problems of the world, refusing to act because the situations or the people involved are disagreeable. Those should be the very situations that spur us on. The nastier the water, the more valuable it is to have a boat.

Being governor led me to depend on faith with a new sense of urgency. I faced situations every day that would have been insurmountable without using the faith God has given me to make decisions.

Less than a month after I took office, I had to decide whether to sign the order for a convicted murderer to be executed. The night of an execution is the loneliest night of a governor's life. I had always favored the death penalty. I could speak about it freely, often gave speeches in favor of it, and even delivered sermons from the pulpit on the subject. I was quite comfortable defending it biblically as well as politically.

But there is a difference between abstract, hypothetical discussion and affixing your signature to set in motion the process by which an inmate will have his life terminated. I sat in the east conference room of the governor's mansion with an open line to the death chamber. Each step of the process was described to me. "They are bringing him into the death chamber now. They're strapping him to the gurney. . . ." For about two hours we kept an open line to see if there was any change from the Supreme Court or a stay from the federal court.

Finally, the moment came when the warden got on the phone and said, "Governor, the prisoner is now prepared. The IV is inserted. Is there any reason we should not proceed?" What came out of my mouth in the next few moments would mean either the life or death of a man. I alone had the power to stop the proceedings or to say, "Proceed," and to know that within four to twelve minutes, a human being would be dead.

I cannot describe what that was like. I could not have prepared myself for it. I authorized other executions after that one, but it never became any easier. If it had, there would have been something terribly wrong with either me or the process. I took my action with a sense of resolve, and to this day I am confident that I did the right thing—"right" defined against moral absolutes in the midst of an imperfect world.

In an ideal world, this man would never have committed the horrible murders for which he was tried and found guilty. The process was both tedious and thorough. He had every opportunity to appeal. He was found guilty and sentenced to die. Nevertheless, the moment a governor gives the order to proceed, he is answering to God for his action and not to the taxpayers.

Thank God for Absolutes

At those critical moments in my life, I thank God for His absolutes. I don't see how anyone could make their decisions otherwise. I've heard spirited debates on the subject, and I find that every one of those who argue against the existence of absolutes have never thought through the logical consequences of their position.

If there are no absolutes—if nothing can be defined as either always right or always wrong—then there must be no God. As one philosopher has said, "If there is no God, then everything is permitted." But if there is a God, there are absolutes.

If there is no God and no absolutes, then nothing is always right and nothing is always wrong. Right and wrong can only be determined by what a majority of the people believe and accept at a certain time and in a certain place, and so it is (in the purest sense) a system in which the majority rules. Whatever the people consent to becomes "right."

If there are no moral absolutes, then the United States had no right to intervene and tell the Third Reich that the annihilation of Jews was wrong. After all, if there are no absolutes, then the majority rules—and by definition, their decision must be right. "But," people may argue, "we all know that is wrong."

But how do we all know any such thing? How can something be wrong if the majority assents to it and has the power to enforce it? In such cases, the logic of relativism disappears. No one can live for long with a system that disallows God and moral absolutes, because no one can live with the consequences if they follow relativism to its natural conclusion.

Or consider another example. Why do we care about victims of natural disasters? After all, it wasn't *our* house that was destroyed. Answer: Because we "feel something."

And why do we "feel something"? Is it social pressure? If so, we can shake that off. Or do we "feel something" because we have a conscience? And if we have a conscience, where did it come from? Where does the moral compass come from that makes us want to show compassion, to give of ourselves, to believe there is something better?

Relativism is an enormous stumbling block to the governments of atheistic countries. I once heard that the Chinese ambassador to the United Nations accused America of trying to impose its human rights standards unfairly on the Chinese people. He said Chinese standards were different, and he's right. "Chinese standards" of human rights have caused unimaginable death and suffering through the years. Adherence to God's immovable standard in that nation would result in new hope and new opportunities for more than a billion of the world's people. But where there are no absolutes, the leadership is free to set whatever standards it likes.

The Consequences of Drifting

Everyone has friends who have faced harsh consequences after drifting from their moral center. Dick Morris conducted opinion polls for me when I was lieutenant governor. I found him to be a fascinating individual. We could hardly be more different. He's a classic New Yorker, reared in Manhattan, the son of a prominent attorney. I was born in Hope, Arkansas. My father was a fireman, and I went to a small Baptist university.

As a person to track public opinion, he was ideal. Someone who thinks and acts the same way I do will only reinforce my own opinions. In a political campaign, Dick could test all of our political ideas and policy positions. You don't really know if your position is defensible until you know you can sell it to people who are not like you. In politics, it's tempting to surround yourself with people who think the same way you do, but that can be dangerous. On the other hand, you don't want to surround yourself with people who can manipulate you. Dick could be dangerous to a person who didn't know what he believed. If you weren't secure in your convictions, he could soon have you believing what he believed.

We had a lot of arguments, but I learned a great deal from him about how to shape and communicate my ideas. He was a brilliant political strategist.

Yet the whole country learned that Dick was having an extramarital affair. How could it have happened? In my view, it was the result of his never embracing a moral center. He had no fixed reference point, no immovable absolute. He substituted his own standards of relative morality for true morality, and the result came back to haunt him.

Whether it's in public policy or with friends, Christians have opportunities every day to put their faith to work. Take your faith off the trailer and head out into the murky waters of daily obstacles and challenges. That's what it was built for.

12
DECISIONS, DECISIONS

As governor, I spent a large part of my day making decisions about issues that affected other people's lives. I even had to make decisions about which decisions to make.

The first step was to separate the immediate from the ultimate. Everybody's needs are immediate, but they aren't all ultimate. Everyone believes his or her needs are the most important things in the world. The tough part of my job was having to decide in what part of the food chain a particular issue lay. Usually, it wasn't anywhere close to where the parties involved thought it was. When I made a decision based on such a judgment, people were bound to be disappointed. But the job required it.

Next, I would ask how great an impact the issue would have. How many people were involved? How wide an area was affected? How much money was involved? Did it have long-term consequences? If you were to tell me there was a bird about to be killed outside, I knew that if the bird died, it died, and that was that. But if you told me there was a disease out there that could affect every bird that flew, that was more important. I had to examine the facts and decide if it was an isolated incident or an ongoing problem. Was it an avalanche rolling down the side of the mountain, or was it a single snowball that had already been thrown and had melted? I had to separate the big from the small.

Dr. Vester Wolber was a professor of religion when I attended Ouachita and was one of the wisest people I have ever met. He had a lot of little sayings, one of which was, "Don't use all your water to put out too small a fire." Sometimes we overreact to something others perceive as a crisis and use all the water we have to put out a small fire. Then when the bigger ones come, we have no resources left. That kind of temptation could get someone in my position in trouble. If you allowed them to, persuasive, well-meaning people would drain every ounce of energy you had for something that didn't deserve it. I had to say no constantly.

I had a staffer in charge of handling problems in our 311 school districts. When she found one, getting it solved was the most important issue of the day. But I had hundreds of boards and agencies, 53,000 employees, and 2.5 million bosses. And the other 310 school districts had problems, too. Sometimes I had to say, "I understand your concern and I appreciate your work, but I have other concerns as well. That is why I am not going to spend three hours talking to that third-grade teacher." It's not that I didn't care, but I didn't have three hours to give to it. Making a call like that was part of the job. I used my lists to decide which issue to consider next.

Another saying I like is that "the difference between successful people and failures is that successful people are willing to do the things failures don't like to do." When you make your list, if you go back and pick out the things that aren't pleasant and do them first, you'll get a lot more done. Most people do the opposite. They take care of tasks they enjoy first, make sure the fun stuff takes up all their time, and leave the rest of their tasks undone. Then they rationalize by saying, "I was going to do these things, but I ran out of time." It's like the child who tries to get out of cleaning his room by saying there was an educational program on TV he "had to watch."

Another goal is to make "duty" decisions only once. For example, if you say, "I'm going to join a church," don't wake up Sunday morning and spend thirty minutes debating whether or not you're going. Don't waste time dealing with decisions you've already made. If you say, "I'm going to abstain from sex until I get married," then don't struggle with it every time you go on a date. You've already decided that, and it's now your duty.

How to Choose Employees

When considering someone for a job, make sure that person has mastered his current level of responsibility before giving him more. There's always someone who says, "I really need to be a department director. I can manage something bigger. I'm not really fulfilled where I am." If you aren't able to do well where you start, you will probably never go beyond where you start. In fact, you'll probably go below that level.

People who are uncomfortable where they are will not become more comfortable after they get where they want to go. If a person can't be content starting at the bottom, he won't be content at the top. It doesn't matter where you are in the pecking order because your contentment doesn't come from there. It comes from the internal confidence that wherever you are, you're growing and building on your experience to the best of your ability within that system.

Beware of people who judge themselves on the basis of how well somebody else does. Our goal should be to do the best we can. Then we won't begrudge people who are doing better than we are. Nor will we fear that we will be left behind. We're never left behind unless we are worried about being on someone else's track. God has a unique track for all of us. We don't have to run like someone else; we're not supposed to.

How to Settle an Argument

One real challenge is deciding how to settle an argument when both sides have made a good effort to agree, yet have failed to find a compromise and have given up and dug in their heels. The wheels of government can't grind to a halt because two people can't find common ground.

The pathway to resolving what seems to be an irreconcilable disagreement starts with finding out what each party really wants. Often this approach will untangle even the messiest impasse in minutes. Although the two sides think they know what they want, and they may say what they think they want, deep down it may be something else. This is true in marriage, business, and politics. What does each side really want, and what do they need? The need may be different from their stated goals. It may be that their argument is indefensible, but human nature is such that no one ever wants to say, "That was a really stupid idea I've been chasing these past few months."

The solution may be to suggest a graceful way out without the appearance of having suffered a defeat, so that the buyer goes his way saying, "I got it for a low price," while the seller says, "I sold it for a high price," and everyone goes away with what he wanted. The goal is to have both parties thinking they've won.

Most people don't even know what their basic needs are. Suppose that in a marriage, a husband and wife are fighting over money. It's probably not a matter of money; it's an issue of control. It might also be an issue of fear. If the husband grew up not having much money, it may be a fear of returning to poverty. If the wife grew up having a lot of money and then lost it and earned it back, she might be thinking, *Easy come, easy go.*

You need to give each person some confidence in the matter. Make sure that one knows everything is going to be okay: the risk does not mean bankruptcy. At the same time, assure the other that there will be opportunities for risk while still saving money. Once you can determine the real issue, you can work toward a solution in which both parties can feel they've won—not over the other party, but over their own struggles and doubts.

Solving the Unsolvable

While most problems have a solution, some don't. In those cases, you have to be willing to choose your side, confront your opponents, and hold tightly to your position. If you get beat, go down swinging, but absolutely refuse to cave in.

We fought a battle in the legislature regarding a ban on partial-birth abortions. We made it clear: we may lose, but we will never back down. We ultimately won the battle and passed legislation to prohibit this gruesome procedure in Arkansas.

In another piece of state legislation, the General Assembly wanted to control the capital improvements budget and started buying off legislators left and right. I stated throughout, "You may beat us, but you won't buy us." This time we lost, but nobody bought us. There are some lines you cannot cross. Make them clear and stand firm.

Caution is important because once you take that sort of stand, there's more at stake than just the issue. Your character is on the line, too. If you cave in, your credibility will be instantly and permanently gone. No one will trust you again. So make sure the issue is worth going to the wall for.

It all goes back to desire versus duty. We have a duty to accomplish certain things: to uphold the Constitution and to be right and honorable. On the other hand, the desire might be, "I would like to have this office space, this staff, or this function." No one is going to perish if he doesn't satisfy his desire. But he might if you don't fulfill your duty.

No Compromise on Core Convictions

Every decision has consequences. Whatever you do, never compromise your core convictions. I find myself encouraged to compromise every day. You have to know your limits. What line can you absolutely not cross? What level can you absolutely not go beyond? Know what these are and stick to them.

The applications of this principle are endless, but one example comes to mind. As governor, people were always telling me they were my friends and wanted to help. They came with the idea that "I need you to do this for me because I am doing that for you." The easiest trap in the world is to begin to renegotiate your principles just a little bit to pay back a friend or to do something nice for someone who has done something nice for you.

There may be people who are doing things for you with pure motives, but you can never allow yourself to fall into the trap of letting their favors influence your decisions. If you ever let that guard down, you'll be in real trouble. You can be grateful to get what proper favors you receive. But never think for a moment you would have gotten them had you not been governor. Or that you will get them after you leave. You won't.

Some of what I know about making decisions comes from experience, but I hope most of it comes as spiritual wisdom from God. If there is one example I can offer about decision making, it's in my daily reading from Proverbs and my study of the Sermon on the Mount. I have always said that if a person had nothing to read but the Sermon on the Mount and the Book of Proverbs, he would have a more credible basis for management than any book ever written on the subject. I have never been exposed to a principle of good management that I couldn't find in the Sermon on the Mount or the Book of Proverbs. They cut to the heart of how to become a successful manager and why to do it.

My philosophy of life is to take God very seriously, but never to take myself very seriously. Fear God, honor Him, love Him, worship Him, and always remember He is the standard.

He is personified in Jesus Christ; therefore, whatever He says He is, we take that seriously. On the other hand, I do not take myself too seriously. I can't afford to feel self-important or indispensable. Other people have been governor of Arkansas, and more will follow after I'm gone. There isn't a job in this world somebody else hasn't done, will do, and probably will do better. I could compare myself to others, but that is not my standard. My standard is Christ; I will have to answer to Him alone.

The Necessity of Fun

Of course, taking Christ seriously doesn't mean you can't have fun. You must have a sense of humor. You have to blow off some steam. It's tragic that some people are so afraid of enjoying life. To me, humor is a defense. I've read that many comedians are people in deep pain. They often are depressed; they are sometimes lonely and extraordinarily sensitive. Comedy becomes their defense mechanism. It's a way to release tension, relieve their burdens, and shake off depression.

When Norman Mailer had cancer, he went on "humor therapy." He wrote an article called "I Laughed Myself to Health." Scientists now know that laughter releases endorphins into the body, natural pain relievers with almost the same effect as a narcotic.

There is real power in having a sense of humor. Proverbs 17:22 says, "A merry heart doeth good like a medicine, but their bitter spirit dries up the bones." Sometimes the best medicine we can reach for is not a bottle or a pill, but a joke book. The capacity to laugh, to make light of situations that are heavy, is incredibly important. Morticians have their own brand of death humor. Soldiers have their combat humor. They must have that to survive. If you go into your job thinking the whole world is on your shoulders—if you feel that kind of unbearable pressure—you need to release it in some way. And humor is a great way to do it.

The Necessity of Inner Peace

In everything I do, I need to be at peace with myself. If my world were to come crashing down, I don't want to say, "That's the end of everything!" Nothing is more important to me than having peace with myself as a Christian, being in Jesus Christ, and knowing that whatever I do, the potential of grace and forgiveness is there. That doesn't give me license for a life of carelessness! It gives me a sense of direction.

Our goal as Christians is to please Him, to emulate Him. We don't want to displease Him, to try and get away with as much as possible. That would show indifference toward Jesus and disrespect for God, and a person who acts that way clearly doesn't know God.

I'm sure about one thing: I not only want to know Him, I want others to be able to see Him through the decisions I make and by the way I make them.

13
A MEDIUM RARELY WELL DONE

I am not afraid of television. I was doing television by age twenty-one and began hosting my first TV show on our church station in Pine Bluff in 1984. Television is the most powerful tool in history for reaching a large audience, and anyone who expects to shape public policy these days has to be comfortable in front of a camera.

That is not necessarily comforting news to intelligent, capable politicians who despise being on television—but television is the medium of the moment in America. Many people in the public eye forge ahead with their plans, ignoring the power of television and then wonder why no one understands or supports their ideas. Even public figures who successfully withstand television's unblinking gaze often don't make the most of its potential to help them.

Television was an indispensable ally for me on July 15, 1996, when I was able to speak to the whole state and tell Arkansans what was happening with the Jim Guy Tucker debacle. I believe the electronic media are neutral rather than automatically hostile. Television is like fire. Fire can be good or it can be bad. It can burn you, but it also can warm you, cook your food, and purify.

How to Manage the Media

Several points are helpful in dealing with the media. One is to not be afraid. Whether you like it or not, the media provide the vehicle through which whatever you do or say is delivered to people. I had to accept the reality that Arkansans' perceptions of me and what I was doing came through the media.

Second, you must diversify your contacts with various types of media. Never have one reporter or one newspaper be your only contact. Don't become dependent on one medium, either. Some public officials say they want to deal only with television, radio, newspapers, cable, or whatever. That's a mistake; all of them are important.

Today's diversity of media is a great benefit. It used to be that there was a limited number of media you could use to help you project a public image: newspaper, radio, or TV. Now there are new technologies like the Internet. There are newsletters, magazines, trade journals—many ways to communicate a message—and you need to take advantage of them all. If a newspaper doesn't like you, there may be nothing you can do to change that. You have to be ready to counter it with other information outlets.

I doubt there is a politician alive who hasn't had a run-in with a reporter who simply doesn't like him and will always write things with a negative slant. You can't stop such biased reporting, but you can try to circumvent it by finding enough honest reporters to balance those slanted reports.

The Power of Television

There is no question that television has totally changed politics. In fact, I wonder if a man as homely as Lincoln or as big as Taft could be elected president in the television age. I'm sometimes criticized because I use TV and radio frequently. (I had monthly radio and TV programs as governor, so anyone in the state could speak directly with me about concerns he or she had.) Political opponents accuse me of glossing over the issues and say it's "not fair" that I am relaxed and believable on the air. Style shouldn't count, they say.

First of all, style alone has never gotten anybody elected. Second, if the people want to elect a bumbling idiot who can't put a sentence together and appears incredibly nervous on camera, there's nothing to stop them from it. But don't dismiss someone just because he's comfortable talking to people through our society's most effective medium of communication. Such an attitude is like getting mad at someone because he runs the mile faster than you, when running fast is the whole point! If the medium of winning the race is the track, then learn to run on that track. If you're going to be in a football game, learn to grab the ball, hold onto it, and get it to the goal line. If the medium for moving public policy is television, then understand that TV is the field of play and learn to run on it. Don't complain about it. Accept the facts for what they are.

It doesn't mean you have to give up your intellect; it means you have to be able to demonstrate that intellect in the medium the public has chosen. If you can't do that, then you probably aren't going to be successful in politics today.

14
CANDIDATE IN THE MIRROR

Although President Bill Clinton and I obviously differ greatly on political issues, in many ways the president represents what Republicans promote in their public policy: self-determination, setting goals, and overcoming adversity on your own.

Young Bill Clinton was poor and disadvantaged; but from the time he was young, he was focused like a laser on becoming president of the United States. It's what he wanted; it's what he worked for and sacrificed for, and through the years he managed to remove all the barriers to his goal. While there are 300 million Americans who can say whatever they want about him, he was still our nation's forty-second president. In that way, Bill Clinton's rise to success epitomizes the American dream.

"But You Know, I Like Him"

Bill Clinton overcame more than his humble upbringing to become president. The year before the 1992 election, President Bush's approval ratings were through the roof as a result of the Persian Gulf War. Meanwhile, Clinton had to face accusations of extramarital activity, experimental drug use, and even a question of his patriotism during the Vietnam War. His policies on issues such as homosexuality and abortion were anathema to the mainstream evangelical community.

And yet, when it came to making a decision, American voters ended up saying, "But you know, I like him." People were more interested that someone reflect who they were rather than someone they wanted to be or thought they should be. When voters got up in the morning and looked in the mirror, they didn't see fighter pilot, CIA director, China envoy, President Bush. That made them uncomfortable. They were more like that young, flawed, sincere man, Bill Clinton.

A Watershed Year

That sort of thinking—*the president is just like me*—was the gradual result of post-Watergate cynicism. The Nixon administration was vilified because back then we had an idealistic image of a president; we wanted him to be the most honorable, most statesmanlike of all of us. He represented more than himself.

He represented all that was good about our country. We wanted our political leaders to be statesmen, and we thought of them in those terms.

But in the post-Watergate era, cynicism mushroomed. People started not only accepting the worst, but *expecting* the worst from their elected officials.

I became a teenager in 1968, a year I have always considered a watershed date in American history. That year marked the death of innocence: the assassinations of Robert Kennedy and Martin Luther King Jr., the Chicago riots, and the horror of Vietnam. The world didn't change completely in a single year, but in 1968 the shift in our society became too apparent to miss. People were angry. Student protests and the hippie movement were at fever pitch. The Black Panthers came into their own. There was a total loss, not just of innocence, but of a sense of community and wholesomeness. It really did mark a turning point. From that year onward, we have lived in the age of the birth control pill, free love, gay sex, the drug culture, and reckless disregard for standards.

The "turn on, tune in, drop out" movement gave personal debauchery a new license. People felt free to do whatever they wanted. Your norm and my norm became the cultural norm. No longer did we live by the standards of God; it became, "You define your standard, I'll define mine, and everybody will be happy. Nobody can tell me to pray; nobody can tell me to read a Bible; nobody can tell me what is right and wrong. I have to make those decisions for myself." It was the beginning of the

"Me Generation," which mushroomed in the seventies. By the time we got to Watergate, morality had become a joke.

Should We Talk about It?

Not long ago, no reporter would consider running an exposé on a president's personal life. Indiscretion was considered horrendous. You just didn't talk about those things in public. Respect for the office and a sense of public decorum prevented it.

In the 1920s, President Warren G. Harding had numerous mistresses, one of whom bore him a child—but it never hit the front-page news. We thought then that our presidents were better than that. When Franklin Roosevelt died, he was on vacation with a woman other than his wife—a woman he had promised he would not see again. Yet the scandal mill produced no grist. During the sixties, it would have been unthinkable for anyone to publish news of President Kennedy's intimate White House escapades or rto un a photo of Jackie—a heavy smoker—with a Marlboro hanging from her lip. Both public figures and the media were discreet, even about indiscretions.

As forces began chipping away at America's public sense of morality, people became increasingly bold about their lifestyles. Gays proudly came out of the closet. Pushers and users openly discussed drugs and drug addiction. Movie stars all but bragged on television about their affairs and their bouts with alcohol. Divorce lost any kind of stigma as did teen pregnancy.

And what role does the media play in this downward spiral? I believe the media only reflects culture; it doesn't create it. That is one place where I differ from many of my evangelical brothers. The media isn't a light, but a mirror. People buy what they see in themselves. That helps explain why in 1992 we elected Bill Clinton, not George Bush, as president.

Pursuing the American Dream

My purpose in providing this kind of cultural critique is not to depress or anger you, but to urge you to become all you can be for the welfare of our country and for the glory of God. Pursuing such a goal won't be easy in our current culture, but it is possible. President Clinton and I are from the same hometown. We were both born in Hope, Arkansas. We went to the same kindergarten—Miss Marie's—nine years apart, then both attended Brookwood Elementary.

Even though we were born in the same town, we grew up in very different environments. The president has told the story of how he grew up with an abusive, alcoholic stepfather. I was fortunate to grow up without that sort of family tension. My father was a fireman who ran a little machine shop on weekends; my mother was a clerk.

Clinton went to college out of state, then on to England as a Rhodes Scholar. He had a secular educational environment. I went to Ouachita Baptist University, where I came to intellectual grips with my convictions and became comfortable with them beyond my emotions.

Today the former president and I have a cordial, genuinely engaging relationship. He is warm, hospitable, and encouraging to everyone around him. That's one of the reasons he has been so successful. He can make anyone, regardless of who he or she is, feel comfortable and at home. He really enjoys being around people. I admire what he has been able to accomplish.

Of course, this doesn't mean I celebrated the fact that someone with his worldview was governing America; just the opposite. I thought a lot of his decisions on partial-birth abortions, social programs, and other issues were way off the mark. But there were two ways for us to approach that situation. One was to be angry and bitter that he was president. The other was to say, "If he could become president with his disadvantaged background, how many other young Americans could, too?" Let's hope we train some of them to want the same goal.

I honestly hope Clinton's story will inspire others to become leaders, even if they start out in modest circumstances. People can look down on you for being poor or for other reasons, but you don't have to let it get to you. I know what it's like to be left behind, left out, or to be the last one picked. I've been there. (Remember, I'm an Arkansas Republican.) When those sorts of painful things happen, you can either turn inward and retreat or rise above it, look beyond it, and believe in yourself. You have no control over where you start in life, but you do have control over where you finish.

I see kids visit the capitol all the time, just like I did when I first came on a fifth-grade field trip. They walk around, looking up at the high ceilings, eyes open wide. It might as well be the Taj Mahal. It is a beautiful building. The first time, it's an awesome sight. Children would say things to me like, "Are you really the governor?" or "Would you sign my book?" And I would think, *Someday, you could be sitting in this office.*

My favorite time of day as governor was when legislative pages would come in to get their pictures taken or when I would meet with school groups. I always tried to encourage them. Most people think it would be boring to jump from one end of the room to the other for pictures, to stand near the flag, or to give a walk-through of the governor's office. But during those times, I wasn't so much looking at the cameras as I was the kids' faces and seeing how they responded to being there. Looking at it through their eyes made me feel like a kid again. It really excited me. When I walked in as a fifth-grader, I never imagined that one day other fifth-graders would be coming to see *me* in that room.

With that in mind, it's my sincere hope that our culture's moral decline (as reflected in the media) does not discourage bright, young minds from pursuing the American dream. Rather, I hope that the great needs of this country will inspire our kids to become reformers, crusaders, leaders, governors—even presidents.

I know of at least two little boys from Hope, Arkansas, who have found that to be true.

15
THE POLITICS OF PERSONAL DESTRUCTION

President Clinton coined the phrase "politics of personal destruction" during the Whitewater scandal and the subsequent impeachment process. Although he admitted he had lied to a grand jury, the president managed to avoid ouster from office. He did so by appealing to the growing distaste of Americans for a political system in which candidates are portrayed as bad people rather than a system in which competing ideas are debated.

Elective politics is not the only realm in which character assassination takes place. It can be the politics of the business office or the politics of the church. It also can be true of marriage and the family. Many people determine it is better to divorce their partners than to work to develop a deeper intimacy.

Even by the standards of Jesus, it is not wrong to have enemies. But it is wrong to hate them. Jesus had enemies. Most of us find it inevitable as we go through life that we will encounter people who are considered enemies. President Lincoln said that we should love our enemies because they are the only ones who will always tell us the truth.

It is easy to love our friends. But loving our enemies requires an extraordinary touch of grace and a true understanding of what love means. Loving our enemies does not mean giving in to their demands or compromising our values. Actually, none of us has the capacity to control the actions of others. But we are responsible for our reactions to the behavior of others.

Loving Our Enemies

One of the most misunderstood admonitions of the Bible is the instruction on dealing with bad behavior that is directed toward us. The ancient code of retaliation known as "an eye for an eye" (Exod. 21:24) is actually a marked improvement over the more barbaric attitude, "Cut out my eye ,and I will cut off your head."

Most of our hearts are ruled more by a sense of revenge than by a sense of justice. Revenge is a drive that is natural to us. We want more than just getting even. Jesus cited three examples of unfair actions that we might encounter. If we are struck on the right cheek, we are to turn the other cheek. If we are sued for our coat, we are admonished to give it up voluntarily. And if we are forced to do a duty that we don't want to do, we are encouraged to go the "second mile"—to do more than required (see Matt. 5:39–42).

In the ancient culture in which Jesus lived, a strike on the right cheek was an insulting blow to a person's dignity and pride. The coat represented people's legitimate possessions, which were necessary for covering and warmth. And the first mile a person was compelled to travel was his or her duty under the Roman legal code.

Jesus set new standards by telling us we should never be content to do only what is expected of us. We should go to the next level by living and giving beyond our obligations and expectations. The way to win over an enemy is not to conquer but to serve. When a person goes beyond the expected duties and responsibilities, he or she demonstrates higher qualities of excellence, leadership, and accomplishment.

Getting ahead today often means disabling others so they are unable to complete the race. But such an approach does not represent getting ahead at all. There is no honor in such a victory—only shame. When the associates and husband of former Olympic skater Tonya Harding were accused of attacking competitor Nancy Kerrigan, the world was repulsed. Without able and honorable competition, victory in any endeavor is meaningless.

The restaurant that eliminates a competitor across the street by starting a whispering campaign about people getting food poisoning at that eatery might succeed for a time. Ultimately, though, quality and service of the surviving restaurant will decline without competition.

Loving others is not the same as performing according to the demands of others. We do not truly love an alcoholic by giving him what he craves—another drink. True love must draw the line and say "no." Genuinely caring about another person does not necessarily mean doing what that person demands. By the same token, *eliminating* competition is not nearly as productive in the long term as *besting* the competition. A basketball team that never plays a game but advances due to the forfeiture of other teams is not prepared to play its best. A politician who seeks to win an election by destroying the reputation of his opponents will eventually die by the sword.

Healthy, Head-to Head Competition

Our goal should be living for the ultimate—living beyond our lifetime. This requires that we think not in terms of getting rid of those who oppose us. Instead, we should overcome them with superior ideas and values. The most effective way to prove that one car is better than another on the track is not to let the air out of the tires of the competition.

People whose principles are well grounded are not afraid of competition. Elijah challenged the prophets of Baal on Mount Carmel. After inviting them to call upon their pagan god to consume a sacrifice on the altar, he called upon the living God to do the same (1 Kings 18:20–39). It is a big mistake for people of integrity and faith to believe that they advance their cause by destroying the competition.

If you believe your faith leads to God, then let others see God's qualities in you. Do you believe your business offers the best products at the best prices? Then let satisfied customers become your unofficial and most effective sales force. Do you believe your candidate is the best for the job and would serve most effectively? Then push the platform of that candidate rather than attacking opponents.

When promises made become promises kept, the public will have confidence. It has been my experience that people are more willing to accept a candidate whose acts are consistent with his stated convictions than one who spouts the popular view but never succeeds in translating that view into positive results.

General Robert E. Lee was once asked to give his opinion of a man who had spoken ill of him on many occasions. Lee spoke kindly of the man. One of his aides could stand it no longer and spoke up. "General, you have spoken very kindly of this individual, but he has taken every opportunity to speak hatefully about you," he said. "Why would you say such nice things about him?"

Lee replied, "I was asked my opinion of *him*, not his opinion of me."

We need more people who can engage in issues of importance while remaining on the high road, avoiding the ditches of personal destruction. Some wag observed that contemporary politics is like a demolition derby, and that whoever is still standing at the finish line will be the winner. For the sake of public civility, we must convince people that winning ultimately is more important than winning immediately.

Not only is it inevitable to have enemies; it may be desirable. Enemies can provide the necessary traction for one's principles. They help us learn perseverance and teach us to love people who are not very lovable. The challenge of living beyond our lifetime begins with being more than a critic of what is wrong. We must strive to be a creator of what is right.

The people who scream "kill the umpire" tend to be those who are sitting in the cheapest seats in the park. I am amused whenever I listen to sports talk shows on the radio. It is apparent that people who have never played a down of football are capable of giving a detailed analysis of what is wrong with the team and comment on how various players have failed to perform adequately. These are people whose qualifications consist of watching sports on television while consuming their weight in potato chips and beer. Truly successful people are more critical of themselves than they are of others.

I have become increasingly amused by editorial writers and self-appointed political reformers who think they know how to solve all the problems faced by the government. They are not subject to the levels of disclosure they demand of elected officials. They have never had to implement decisions in the complex world of partisan politics—a world that is open to public scrutiny.

My family has had to endure attacks I never would have imagined before running for office. Frivolous lawsuits instigated by political opponents who are unable to find real issues can create distractions from the tasks at hand. Some members of the media are willing to take baseless allegations and not only report them but repeat them over and over.

Although attacking others will sometimes work with voters, it will not work as we stand before God's judgment seat. He will judge based on what he knows, not on what our critics have said about us.

16
WINNING AN ELECTION, LOSING A GENERATION

Politics has always been a contact sport. It has increasingly become a demolition derby, with each contestant entering the arena and then engaging in a series of crashes. Whoever remains standing is declared the winner. The best person with the superior ideas is often less important than the most creative advertising campaign and the largest war chest. Add in the cynicism of the media and the fact that so many political opponents are willing to play hardball. All of this means that running for public office is certainly not for the faint of heart.

I may not always like the process of politics, but the end product is public policies that lay the track upon which the next generation will move forward. No matter how idealistic a person is when entering the political arena, I can attest from personal experience that there's always a temptation to make decisions that will affect the next election rather than chart the best course for the next generation. It's easy to justify such an attitude by telling yourself that if you don't get reelected, you won't be able to have an impact on future policy development. Our society increasingly demands measurable results in a short time. Being in public office is now about building a résumé of accomplishments rather than laying the foundation for a lasting legacy that will result in a lifetime of change.

Doing It for the Children

As governor, I tried to visit public schools, preferably elementary schools, as often as possible. One of my primary reasons for visiting schools was not so much to introduce the students to a governor as it was to help remind me of what's really important about being in public office. My batteries are recharged when I'm around children. They are still filled with awe and wonder. They have not become like so many adults—angry, distrustful of others, filled with doubt and broken dreams.

Not long after becoming governor in 1996, I sat in a meeting room at a Little Rock hospital with almost fifty representatives of organizations that received Medicaid funds. We had asked them to assist us in finding areas in which we could save money in the Medicaid system. The state was rapidly approaching the point at which the needs would exceed the funding levels.

I listened for more than an hour as participants talked about the virtues of their organizations and why they needed to be given even more money. In a meeting designed to ask the participants how they could live with less, each found a way to articulate how he or she couldn't live without more.

I called on a quiet lady across the room who lifted her hand to be recognized. What she said in the next few minutes stirred something in me that would change my views and the agenda for tens of thousands of Arkansas children. She was Amy Rossi, executive director of Arkansas Advocates for Children and Families. She was known by regulars at the state capitol as a well-meaning person who tried to influence legislation so it would have more of a positive effect on children, especially those from poor families.

I had heard from people who wanted more tax dollars for their organizations, but her plea was refreshingly different. She wasn't there to ask for more money for an organization. She was there to remind us of a serious need in our state. She spoke passionately about the 110,000 Arkansas children whose parents were working and had avoided welfare, but whose income was not enough to afford adequate health insurance for their children.

Those kids fell into an unfair trap. They were the children of parents who earned too much to qualify for Medicaid and not enough to afford quality private health insurance plans.

They were children whose chronic illnesses often were going undiagnosed and untreated.

Amy's plea might have been filed away with the other good ideas I regularly heard as governor, but I couldn't stop thinking about those children. I realized the only thing that separated them and me was forty years. Fortunately for me and my family, the cost of insurance and medical care was not nearly as high in the 1950s and 1960s as it is now. It occurred to me that many children were perhaps being penalized because their parents had worked their way above the poverty line.

Subsequent meetings with the director of the Arkansas Department of Human Services, Tom Dalton, and state Medicaid director Ray Hanley brought forth a simple but revolutionary idea that gave the children of working parents preventive care. The ARKids First program was born. I introduced it to the Arkansas legislature in January 1997. It passed without a negative vote in either the House or the Senate.

I remember coming up with the name of the program while seated at my desk at the state capitol, feeling a true sense of inspiration. When the legislation was approved, I had the pleasure of signing the bill while seated at a small table surrounded by children at a downtown Little Rock day care center. The children were drawing pictures with crayons.

As I prepared to sign the bill, I found myself reaching for one of the crayons and probably made history by being the first person to sign a bill into law with a crayon rather than a pen. The spontaneity of the moment took hold, and the crayon became one of the symbols of the plan.

Since its conception in 1997, the ARKids First program has been incredibly successful in insuring more than sixty thousand children whose families probably could not have otherwise afforded preventive health care. By the time Congress passed its own children's health initiative months later, our program was up and running. Many of our citizens actually welcomed the small copayment that was required since it gave them a sense of shared responsibility and a feeling of not being "on welfare."

The real value of ARKids First will not be seen immediately, but I'm convinced it's less expensive to prevent a problem than it is to try to fix it once it has grown into something much larger. The value of ARKids First will be easier to see over the decades as children grow up having not missed school because of chronic illnesses. Is it costly? It's not as costly as having large numbers of sick children.

Thinking Bigger than an Election Cycle

Another initiative we promoted heavily in Arkansas was the Smart Start program, which puts a major emphasis on high standards and accountability while focusing on reading, math, and character-based education in the early grades. With Arkansas consistently ranked near the bottom in educational achievement, creating and implementing a statewide initiative that refocuses public education is an important task.

Like the ARKids First program, the real value of Smart Start will not be most notably evident in the short-term. It will take more than a single school year to see what happens when children grow up in a public education system where there are no excuses for failure, where the standards are raised instead of lowered, and where individual students and schools are held accountable.

There is a temptation among public officials to implement programs with an eye toward short-term results. This is an age of "micropolicies," the launching of which provide colorful backdrops for television cameras. Most of these programs do little in the long run to improve our country.

The longer I served as governor, the more I tried to remind myself that my most important decisions were not those that would affect the next election but those that would affect the next generation. If public officials had fought for generational programs fifty years ago, my state might not be one of the poorest in the country. The politics of "right now" too often has robbed our citizens of the changes needed to make their lives better.

Our Arkansas prison system is one of the most efficient in the country in terms of cost. We spend far below the national average. But consider that for the same amount of money we spend to keep someone in a prison, we could enroll a student in any college or university in the state, pay full tuition, pay room and board, buy books, and still provide some spending money. Few things grieve me more than having to build more prisons to meet the demand that drugs and crime have placed on the Arkansas Department of Correction.

I can't help but wonder how many people who languish in our prisons today might have been learning in our colleges and universities if we had placed a higher priority on building a fence at the top of the hill to keep them from falling off. This would have been preferable to spending big money on ambulances at the bottom of the hill to pick up what was left after they fell.

I was determined during my tenure in office as governor to fight the demons of instant gratification, adopting policies that might not have an immediate result but would help the people of my state beyond my lifetime.

Not everyone governs a state. But everyone makes decisions that affect others. Just as politicians are tempted to live only for the next election, many Americans live for the next vacation or even the next weekend. In a culture that's addicted to pleasure and immediate gratification, it's increasingly difficult to live in a way that will impact lives long after we're gone.

Deeply-Rooted Principles

A young man rapidly approached his birthday and could sense something significant was going on. A week before his birthday party, he found the garage door locked. On his birthday, he was escorted to the kitchen, where he was met by his parents, grandparents, and a number of aunts and uncles. The family then gathered near the garage door and watched as the boy's father placed the key in the padlock and opened the door.

A large section of a tree—more than five feet tall and at least a foot thick—greeted the boy and his family. As he approached the tree, he noticed it had been meticulously polished. He also noticed small signs that noted the dates at which rings of the tree had formed and the connection to events in history. One ring was labeled "The Emancipation Proclamation, 1863." Another marker showed the year when his mother and father had married.

As the boy studied the rings, he learned about the history of his family and also gained clues about the history of his race. The boy had been given something far more valuable than a piece of a tree. This gift taught him about his past.

The boy's name was Alex Haley, who grew up to write the best-selling novel *Roots*. This book was adapted into the most significant television miniseries in our country's history.

As we work, rear our children, and make daily decisions, we need to ask if they are for the immediate or for the ultimate good. Imagine the difference in government alone if we made decisions based on how they impacted the next generation rather than influenced the next election.

17
LET IT SHINE

I hear one comment a lot these days: "Now that you've been governor, I guess you want to be the next guy from Arkansas to go to the White House."

If I really wanted to move up to the next level, I'd have plenty of company. There are 135 people in the Arkansas state legislature who think they could be governor. There are probably 50 governors who think they could be president; there are 100 senators and 435 members of the House who think the same thing. Wherever you are, there's a temptation to want to jump to the next level.

I have come to realize that my next position might be at quite a different level. It may be running a soup kitchen somewhere. I'd rather be doing something I know I'm supposed to do than something everybody tells me is right. If you're the governor of a state, there aren't many jobs you can take in that state that people will think are more important.

The great, liberating comfort for me and other believers is that God, not man, is in control, and He knows what is best for me. I am not to be so ambitious that I start thinking I know better than God what's best for me. That's not to say ambition is bad; everybody should have some ambition and strive to do his best. But I could run a marina and tackle shop at Lake Greeson near Murfreesboro and be quite content.

Following God's Lead

I've truly enjoyed doing everything I've ever done. I enjoyed pastoring a small church, serving as director of communications for a Christian ministry, as well as doing advertising, public relations, and promotional work. I enjoyed pastoring a church that grew from a small, struggling group to a large congregation.

Still, being governor of Arkansas was the most fulfilling, challenging, satisfying, and wonderful job I've had. I wouldn't trade the experience for anything. On the other hand, it didn't make me any happier or make me feel any more important than when I was twenty-five years old and pastoring a struggling church in a declining neighborhood. I didn't feel any better living in the governor's mansion than I did living in a forty-dollars-a-month duplex with Janet when we were married as eighteen-year-old college students. We were just as happy in a lot of ways.

Certainly my surroundings as governor were more attractive than they once were. I was exposed to Persian rugs and fine pieces of art on loan from the Arkansas Arts Center. Somebody shined my shoes every night; I just set them outside the bedroom door. My clothes were freshly pressed; my meals were prepared; the beds were made; and other people placed my phone calls and drove me to work. It was all quite convenient, and I appreciated it. But I was just as happy without it.

I think that is the ultimate joy. Like the apostle Paul, I can rejoice because I have seen both plenty and want. They're both interesting, and I can learn a lot from both positions. Persian rugs are nice, but I've been at the bottom, too. I know firsthand that life is good even down there.

Though I've been happy in all of my careers, I freely admit I love the excitement of campaigning. It's the thrill of the unknown. The frantic pace. Some of us are crazy enough to enjoy it; others see it as a necessary evil. George Bush had great disdain for campaigning. Bill Clinton, on the other hand, was very much in my same camp in this regard. We both like people, and in campaigning, the ultimate goal is to be with people—to share your views, listen, sympathize, and persuade. There's also the sense that you always have to be at a peak performance level. You never know when you'll slip. Anybody who campaigns with the assumption that the election is in the bag is living dangerously.

My years in the pastorate and in politics have reinforced my conviction that the most destructive forces in the world are not "out there" somewhere, but inside our hearts. By the same token, the most constructive forces in the world are not out there; they're internal. It always comes back to the fact that character is the most constructive force in the world.

Anyone in a position of responsibility can be eaten up with doubts and second-guessing. His weakness can cause him to accept bad advice with devastating results. But if you have integrity of character, you never have to second-guess, never have to feel guilty, never have to avoid looking people in the eye. The worst thing you can do is lose, and even then you can do so with honor.

On the other hand, if you don't embrace integrity of character, if you can't be at peace with yourself, if you are constantly at war with your soul and you have never resolved who you really are or what you believe in, then you can overcome every problem in the world, but you will only be dishonored and miserable in the end.

Only One Will Prevail

I see a growing polarization in our society. Sometimes it appears as though we are moving toward a more virtuous culture; at other times, I'd swear we are moving toward utter chaos. I see this polarization in politics, the arts, business, and education. People are beginning to move worlds apart and find it increasingly difficult to establish common ground.

Two opposing worldviews account for this polarization. One puts man at the center; the other puts God at the center. The two are absolutely *irreconcilable*. Consensus cannot be reached because the two sides do not even have a basis of agreement with which to begin a discussion.

One of the biggest faults of modern Christians is trying to reconcile a self-centered worldview with Christianity. It is impossible. I see people on one side who have deep Christian convictions; they will become more focused on character. Those on the other side will move steadily toward self-satisfaction.

The two major political parties in America have become polarized as well. Years ago it was a difficult task to pin down the ideological differences between a Republican and a Democrat in Arkansas. There were liberal Republicans and conservative Democrats, especially in the South. Party labels had more to do with social standing than ideology. That's no longer the case. You will now find very wealthy and very poor in both parties, and a distinct ideological separation.

Here's the bottom line, not just for Arkansas and America, but for the world: one worldview will prevail. Either by the force of numbers or persuasion, one side of this polarized culture will defeat the other in setting public policy. When two irreconcilable views emerge, one is going to dominate. Ours will either be a worldview with humans at the center or with God at the center. Standards of right and wrong are either what we establish as human beings (standards which can be changed to suit us), or they are what God has set in motion since the creation of the world and cannot be moved.

This clash is going to occur between those who think man is basically good (if he has enough education and economic parity with his brother, he will do good things and avoid crime, poverty, and disease) and those who say man is basically self-centered (he'll do whatever he can get away with unless his nature is changed by a supernatural act of God, or he is so shamed by the consequences of doing wrong that he is constrained to do right). The winning worldview will dominate public policy, the laws we make, and every other detail of our existence.

For example, if I believe man is basically good, then when I see that we have a high rate of teen pregnancy I will think, *If only people had education and economic parity, it wouldn't happen. I'll create a program that brings sex education to young women and young men and make provisions for birth control. I'm going to spend money and provide education for the people.*

On the other hand, if I believe man is basically self-centered, then I'm going to create consequences for those actions. Instead of saying, "We're going to give you a book" or "We're going to give you a check," I'm going to say, "If you get pregnant, you are going to have a child to care for and support. You aren't going to live as comfortable a life."

How can we change a drug-addicted culture? Do we say, "If these people weren't poor, or if they only knew what drugs did, then they wouldn't be doing this"? If so, you'd prepare a bunch of informational videos and explain the danger. And in fact, that is just what much of government has been doing. And has it worked? No. Will it ever work? No. Why not? Because taking drugs appeals to the self-centered, pleasure-seeking people we are by nature.

If we're convinced of that selfish nature, we take a different tack: "If you use drugs, we're going to put you in jail for so long you won't even remember where you live. We are going to confiscate drugs. We're going to take your car, and if we catch you dealing, we're going to try you and convict you and take away your liberty."

We must come to see that our core problem is not lack of education but lack of righteousness. We don't need more information as much as we need new hearts.

Welfare, abortion, sexually transmitted diseases—every public issue is going to be approached differently depending on which worldview wins out. We aren't talking about degrees of difference; we're talking about one or the other with no ground in between. When I hear people say, "I don't think Christians (or "pastors" or "Baptists" or whatever) ought to get into politics," I respond, "If the Christian worldview does not prevail, the public policy that will teach your children and grandchildren—the policy that will rule their society as well as yours—will be formed by people who think your beliefs fell off the edge of the flat earth. They will defame what you respect and discount your reason for believing it. They will dismiss with rancor everything you think is important."

Is that what you're willing to settle for?

It's not that we want to impose our religion on somebody. It's that we want to shape the culture and laws by using a world-view we believe has value. Both sides believe in their respective position, but both can't be right.

A Candle in the Darkness

Can you make a difference in the battle between a God-centered worldview and a human-centered one? Can your little sputtering light of God-focused character do anything against the looming darkness of a lost world?

I learned the answer the summer before my senior year in high school. That year I went to Expo '72, the first worldwide evangelism conference staged by Campus Crusade for Christ. On the last night of the conference, Billy Graham spoke to almost one hundred thousand young people from all over the world in the Cotton Bowl in Dallas. His message was, "You can touch the world. One person can make a difference."

At the end of his message, the stadium lights went out, and the whole place went black. I was sitting at the other end of the stadium from Dr. Graham. Even at such a distance, with that vast darkness all around, I could see when he lit his candle. One tiny match brought the whole stadium from darkness into light. Graham used his candle to light another held by Bill Bright, the founder of Campus Crusade. The two men lit two other people's candles, making four candles in all; they each lit another candle, making eight.

Everyone in the stadium had been given a candle. As the people up front lit the candles of eight people in the audience, the light spread exponentially. Within a few minutes, one hundred thousand candles, all taking their light from that one candle in Billy Graham's hand, were so bright that people were calling the Dallas Fire Department and reporting the Cotton Bowl on fire. It was an incredible sight. And I realized, more than anything, that the darker things are, the more difference even the tiniest light will make.

Across the room from me there's a night light that stays plugged in all the time. I can't see it now. But if I were to turn off all the lights in this room, your eyes would focus on that little light. The darker it is in here, the more brilliant that tiny bulb will seem. It will penetrate the darkness. The darkness, no matter how great, can never swallow even the smallest light. All the darkness in the Cotton Bowl couldn't quench a single match.

Your spiritual light—your light of integrity, character, and a God-centered worldview—is just as invincible. We live in a dark spiritual age—all the more reason for you to hold your candle high and hold it out to others! The darker the world gets, the brighter your light will shine.

PART III

SELECTED SPEECHES AND COMMENTARY

APPENDIX 1
THE SPEECH THAT NEVER WAS

*This speech was prepared by Lieutenant Governor Hucka-
bee to be delivered on a statewide television broadcast after
his inauguration as governor of Arkansas on July 15, 1996.
He had just finished rehearsing it when Governor Jim Guy
Tucker called to say he had decided not to resign.*

At two o'clock this afternoon, I took the oath of office to
become your governor. The responsibility that has been thrust
upon me and entrusted to me is one that I approach with
unapologetic dependence upon the Spirit of God to give me
the heart of a servant, wisdom for the difficult decisions I will
face each day, the courage to stand by my convictions, and the
humility to acknowledge my mistakes, of which there will be
many.

A few weeks ago, when a jury of our fellow Arkansans patiently reached a verdict in a nearby federal courthouse, our state was shattered emotionally and politically. My decision to withdraw from the race for the United States Senate and to concentrate wholeheartedly on serving as your governor is one I do not regret. I want to help restore Arkansas' image to America as a place of natural beauty, hard-working people, and a family-friendly atmosphere. . . .

While so much attention is focused upon us, I ask every fellow Arkansan to join me in ensuring that America and the world come to know the Arkansas we know and love. Let's make sure the nation sees our real strengths: Nature. Family. Community. We're the kind of folks who take food to a sick friend, put an arm around the shoulder of one who grieves, and who speak a sincere and friendly greeting to those we meet.

Our transition team has been nothing short of amazing during the past seven weeks. With limited resources and time, literally hundreds of Arkansas citizens volunteered and came aboard to help make sure that the people's business would be treated with care. My deepest thanks and utmost praise go to everyone who has worked to prepare for a new beginning in Arkansas.

You may want to know more about your new first family. Janet, my wife of twenty-two years, has been the love of my life since our senior year of high school in our hometown of Hope. You may end up not caring much for me, but you're going to love your first lady. She's a great wife and mother, but most of all, she's a most unpretentious person who can charm guests at a formal reception but is just as comfortable shooting basketball with a high school team, bungee jumping, or making snow cones in a PTA concession booth. We have three teenage children, and that's reason enough to be patient with us. Our oldest son, John Mark, will be a sophomore at Ouachita Baptist University this fall. David is 16, and Sarah turns 14 this summer, and we'll be enrolling both of them in the Little Rock public school system as soon as we get settled.

You're entitled to ask, "What kind of governor will you be?" I plan to be guided by certain principles that will form the basis of policies enabling *every* Arkansas citizen to claim our state truly as the "Land of Opportunity."

1. Those of us elected or employed to serve the citizens need to remember who the boss is. The people who walk through our doors or who call us on our phones are not "nuisances," "irritations," or even "customers." We need to treat them like the boss, because we work for them. They pay for the government we give them. And the owners have a right to be treated with dignity, courtesy, and efficiency. Government was created to serve its people; its people were not created to serve government.

A few weeks ago a reporter cynically asked, "What qualifications or credentials do these so-called volunteers on your transition team have that gives them the right to do this job of going to state agencies and gathering information?" I realized that the reporter's attitude was a perfect reflection of the lack of respect for anyone not part of a self-perpetuating political establishment. Well, the qualifications and credentials of our citizens to examine their government are quite simple—they own it. They pay the full freight because before government can do something for us, it must first take something from us. My goal as governor will not be to see how much money we can collect in the state treasury but how we can raise the standard of living of a working family by leaving more in their pockets in the first place.

2. Government should not penalize productivity and subsidize irresponsibility. Welfare that goes to able-bodied adults should be conditioned upon work and should be a temporary hand up instead of a permanent handout. Let's remember that the burdens of teenage pregnancy should not fall only on the mother or the taxpayers. The father should be required to pay for doctor bills, diapers, and putting food on the table.

3. Let's establish policies for the family built on the premise that when given a strong family-friendly culture, mothers and fathers raise better children than governments do.

4. I believe that a good leader never asks of others what one is unwilling to do himself. To put that into practice, I have issued a directive this morning for all of the staff in my office whose decisions affect policy to spend no less than half a day every eight weeks away from their desks and on the job with someone in state government who actually has to carry out the policies. This directive will start *right* here—with *this* governor—and extend to all the areas of the executive branch over which I have control. We will discover that the best solutions for increasing the quality of your government will come from places other than the Capitol.

5. Government should actually welcome the participation of citizens from the private sector. After all, if a government agency is doing all it can to run efficiently, it should be delighted to have others view its performance. A few months ago here in Arkansas, a non-partisan, independent, volunteer, citizens task force was conceived. The Murphy Commission, led by El Dorado businessman Madison Murphy, has signed more than one hundred professional and business leaders from throughout the state who have committed to developing recommendations to streamline state government and make it more accountable. They will seek to examine the role and functions of state government, including its structure and budgeting and spending process. This kind of partnership can create synergy, giving the private sector insight into the complexities of government and the public sector a chance to help solve problems. Earlier today, I issued a directive to our state agencies, instructing them to give the Murphy Commission access and assistance. This commission must be a team effort and present to me, the Legislature, and the people of Arkansas, practical ways to give our state the highest quality and most cost-effective government in America. The vast majority of our state employees are dedicated public servants who want to do their jobs more efficiently and know how that can be accomplished. When the commission issues its report, I expect that people in the private sector will realize that most waste in the bureaucracy is the result of outdated and cumbersome systems and not personnel. When the recommendations become law, procedure, and policy we will be able to further reduce spending on the *process* and actually provide more useful service for the *people.*

Furthermore, I have issued today a directive to the Department of Finance and Administration to use cost-benefit analysis on all new programs and to continue the hiring freeze for state jobs. My office is asking every agency and department to carefully review the budget requests, to look for every possible cost-saving measure before we begin the process of executive review in the coming weeks. Advocates for each existing program need to demonstrate its effectiveness.

6. I believe the best government is the most local government. This means we need to welcome the growing decentralization of the federal government as states are empowered to match delivery of government services to actual needs. But as one who is neither afraid of nor resistant to such an effort, I recognize two things: First, it means the governor and the legislature must be willing to accept responsibility for the outcomes of our policies. Second, it means that if we merely centralize the power of government at the state level, we haven't gone far enough. More decisions made by county and city leaders, and by local employees of state government is the right way to go.

7. In education, we have succeeded in placing computers in many of our classrooms, but we cannot ignore the need for building character. Knowledge of facts without the wisdom to use those facts for good is like having a computer loaded with data but without the operating system necessary to process the data into usable form. Government's involvement in education should be to establish clear and concise standards developed by citizens and educators throughout our state and to make certain that the resources of our state are distributed fairly among the students and school districts. We will strive to give a greater share of education decisions to classroom teachers, parents, and locally elected school boards. Government should be, above all, a resource, not merely a regulator of education. Most importantly, our schools must provide a safe learning atmosphere with zero tolerance for teenage terrorism.

8. I believe government should facilitate rather than complicate life for those who create jobs by running a business. The philosophy of this governor is that the government has done its job well when our regulations keep people in business by letting them achieve high standards of service and safety instead of running people out of business with over-reaching rules and regulations that cost jobs and profits.

9. Our tax policies should be fair to those who work hard for their paychecks. Ultimately, we need *comprehensive* tax reform, touching all aspects of how we take money from our citizens. Such an approach should ensure that from income tax to property tax, every Arkansan is treated the same, without respect to place, race, or face. One place we can and must start is a responsible, reasonable removal of the sales tax on food. This extremely regressive tax, hitting the lowest-paid working families the hardest, can be eliminated without threatening the future of our children's education, service to our elderly or to the disabled, and without adding unfunded mandates on retailers or threatening city and county budgets. I will be presenting the details of that plan shortly. The broad coalition that supports this tax cut consists of people with a wide variety of political viewpoints.

10. We will prove that when we stop worrying about who gets the credit and focus on what gets done, we can restore the kind of trust in government that has been shattered by the blame-game politics of those who would sacrifice statesmanship for partisanship, principle for personal power, and the next generation for the next election. I have found in my three years in elected office that the overwhelming majority of men and women of the Arkansas General Assembly—both Republicans and Democrats—are honorable people in whom you've placed your trust. You elected them just as you elected me. Cooperation is not optional for us. If we fail to listen to you and refuse to work with each other, you have the right, and even the responsibility, to elect someone else to do the job. I am only the governor. There's little I can do without the partnership of the legislature. When you agree with me, don't just tell me; tell them, too. We will then all be reminded of our state motto: *Regnat Populus* ("The People Rule").

As your new governor, I look forward to working with you to close the cracks of past cronyism and to open wide the windows in this Land of Opportunity. You have my word that

I will give every ounce of my strength to do my duty so as to honor God and faithfully serve the citizens of this great state.

As we enter into this new era of Arkansas history, I truly feel the prayers and goodwill of fellow Arkansans who, regardless of political affiliation, want me to succeed—not just for my sake, but the sake of our state. I will put Arkansas first, and I ask you to do the same. I will daily seek wisdom from God's Word and will ask him for guidance to lead our state as governor. Being governor of Arkansas is an honor I could never have imagined as a small boy growing up under modest circumstances. I only wish my father could have lived just four more months to have witnessed this day. But somehow, I can't help but believe he's watching all of it from the best seat in the house. When I was fifteen years old, a verse from the New Testament—Philippians 4:13—changed my life. It says, "I can do all things through Christ who strengthens me." I'll do my best. And with my family's support, your prayers, and God's help, I can do this job. Janet joins me in saying, "thanks for your friendship," and may God bless our small, but wonderful state.

APPENDIX 2
FACE TO FACE AND
HEART TO HEART

These impromptu remarks were delivered to the Arkansas General Assembly after Governor Tucker notified the lieutenant governor and the General Assembly that he had decided not to resign. Almost an hour after he was supposed to have been sworn in as governor, Lieutenant Governor Huckabee and his wife, Janet, entered the House chamber to a thunderous standing ovation, after which he addressed the assembly.

Is something going on here I need to know about?

I think most of you are now aware of the circumstances which have brought us to this particular moment. I want to say how much I appreciate my wife, Janet, for being with me and for her willingness to stand with me during this very important time.

There was a temptation on my part to simply send a written notification to you, but I felt first of all as a courtesy to you, who had driven from all over the state to be a part of this occasion, because I respect you as elected officials, each representing an important part of our state's population, that it would be inappropriate for me to simply send a written response; and instead, I chose to come and speak to you face to face and heart to heart.

I am grateful for the response, and I wish that it were this way every time I spoke; but I am going to tell you in all candor that this is probably not an occasion that we want to be here longer than necessary, and I would like for us to perhaps hold applause more so for the honor of the people of our state more than anyone of us as individuals.

I was notified by Governor Jim Guy Tucker at 1:55 this afternoon that he intended to rescind his original decision to resign, based on a court motion filed last Friday in Little Rock. Mr. Tucker further indicated his desire to leave the entire matter of his resignation unresolved, despite his earlier promise to resign on or before July 15—without qualifications—in order that he might act in the best interest of the people of Arkansas.

Ladies and gentlemen of this assembled body, this is a very critical moment in our state's history, and it demands that our response is measured with the only concern being that we as elected officials act with the caliber of calm and courage required for such a moment in our history. I would like to request an immediate meeting with the speaker of the House and the president pro tempore of the Senate so that we can gather in my office. It is my intention to fulfill my promise to speak to the state this afternoon at 5:15 on television. The speech may be a little different, but I will be speaking at 5:15.

I realize again that some of you have driven extraordinary distances, you have given up—for many of you who are legislators—a day away from your livelihood, and I want the public to understand, this being informal time, there is not pay or reimbursement for this. I respect more than I can ever tell you the fact that you have come in good faith to witness what we all expected to witness today.

I look forward to meeting with the speaker and the president pro tempore immediately, and I hope you will be able to hear the remarks that I wish to make to all our citizens, including those of you who have been elected to stand tall in a moment like this and be able to represent not what we think or what we hope or believe, but to represent the heart, mind, and the very essence of the people who put us in these very sacred positions of trust.

Thank you, and may God bless you.

APPENDIX 3
OF RIGHT AND WRONG

This speech, completely unscripted and without notes of any kind, was delivered to a statewide television audience at 5:15 p.m. on July 15, 1996. It replaced the previously written and rehearsed speech reproduced in appendix 1.

Good evening, ladies and gentlemen. Tonight I fully expected to address you as the forty-fourth governor of the state of Arkansas. For nearly seven weeks, all of us have anticipated that on or before July 15, our governor would follow through with the promise that he made to the people of our state in late May, when a jury of Arkansas citizens handed down guilty verdicts on two felony counts. The people of Arkansas understood that the governor was acting in the best interest of the people of the state when he chose to step down rather than stay on beyond the period of time which he said would be for an orderly transition.

Tonight, I come here with an extraordinary sense of probably the same shock that you have. I had stayed up late over the past several evenings preparing what was going to be a carefully crafted speech. Needless to say, this afternoon that speech went to the wastebasket. Tonight, I stand before you with no script, with no written words. Just a few moments to share with you from the depths of my heart as a fellow Arkansas citizen exactly where we are at this very critical moment in our state's history.

It was all of our understanding that today was going to be the day in which the governor's announced resignation would take effect. All of us had acted in that regard, both in Governor Tucker's office as well as in my office and with the transition team. We have worked diligently over the past seven weeks, not only in terms of preparing for this moment, but even more so, families have relocated; many people in the governor's office have resigned and taken other positions; others have resigned their work to come to work for me; children have been enrolled in schools; there has been a lot of activity.

But my fellow citizens, let me tell you that this is not about the convenience to anyone. This is far bigger than simple job changes for those of us who have anticipated having to find something or having something find us. What really is at issue tonight is a simple question between right and wrong.

This afternoon, I spent a lot of time listening to legal counsel and experienced people of the law. There are as many opinions as there are lawyers, as you know. But as this afternoon and this hour approached, I realized that this is not a time for a committee decision. What we have to do is come to a place where we take clear and decisive action. Because, frankly, that is exactly what you have elected us to do. Let me give you some of the chronology of what has happened today and how we plan to respond to it.

In the first place, just before two o'clock, approximately 1:55, I received a telephone call from Governor Tucker, indicating to me that he had changed his mind about resigning. Even at this late hour, he indicated that he was drafting and preparing to sign a letter which would simply temporarily give the duties and responsibilities of the governor's office to me in my capacity as lieutenant governor. He further stated that this was based on a motion that he filed in court last Friday, feeling that there was a strong possibility that the motion filed in court could, in fact, result in his jury verdict in May being set aside— further indicating that he felt like, if in fact he did resign and then the court set aside the judgment, he would have resigned in advance of what was appropriate and necessary.

Let me be very candid with you. I have tried very diligently to be cooperative and, frankly, to be very quiet about the actions of the past seven weeks. The literally hundreds of appointments; the nearly $58 million spent in state money. I remained silent because I respected the fact that the governor was still the governor until a court said that he was not. I further knew that on or before July 15, just as he had stated, this issue would be over, and Arkansas could close this chapter of our past and open a brand new chapter for our future. As a result of that, I believe that it was in the best interest of all our people, Democrats or Republicans, to remain as calm as possible and simply to try to stay the course of preparing to become governor. We never imagined that the governor would make any kind of decision like this. I expressed that to him today.

Further, I expressed that in his announcement of resignation in the last part of May, there were no qualifications that he placed on it. Therefore, to add qualifications at this point seemed very inappropriate. As you probably by now know, the House and the Senate were already assembled to be prepared to watch me take the oath of office. In addition to that, there were people gathered all over the Capitol who were prepared for a ceremony at three o'clock. But once again, the issue here is not ceremonies and people's inconveniences—the time they spent driving from Jonesboro, Fayetteville, or Texarkana. The issue is much bigger than that.

Following that session in which we received the governor's letter indicating his refusal to step down from office and merely transfer temporarily the powers of office, I spoke briefly to the House chamber. I was met with an extraordinary sense of warmth and welcome, but more importantly, with the universal support of the members who realize that this is indeed a tragic day for our state, I requested a meeting with Speaker of the House Bobby Hogue and President Pro Tempore of the Senate Stanley Russ. These men are honorable men. I want you to understand that we did not meet as a Republican governor and two Democratic legislators. We met as people who have been charged with the awesome responsibility of making very important decisions.

I know that there are many who will probably say that this is going to be great for the Republicans, isn't it? My friends, this is simply going to be bad for Arkansas. No Republican would ever take pleasure in it, nor should any Democrat be branded with the responsibility of it. The decision that brings us to this crisis was a decision, not of Democrats, not of Republicans, not of the speaker, not of the president pro tempore, or any member elected by you, the people, to serve the Legislature. This was a decision that Mr. Tucker and only Mr. Tucker made. And now this decision will confront the 135 members of the General Assembly and will confront me, who right now stands in the role of acting governor.

Well, I take that seriously. When I swore my oath of office to you, the people of Arkansas, I meant everything I said. Based on my meetings with Speaker Hogue and Senator Russ, the following actions are taking place. I asked Speaker Hogue and Senator Russ to talk with the governor this afternoon. They were dispatched from my office at just about four o'clock. They were to give him the message that we would very much sincerely request that he reconsider his earlier decision and instead would offer to me before five o'clock an unqualified letter of resignation. That offer was refused.

We then said that, if he was unwilling to do it before five o'clock to avoid the further humiliation and the further embarrassment to our state over this issue, we would be forced to take the second course of action. The governor has been notified that as of nine o'clock in the morning, if we have not received from him a letter of unreserved, unqualified resignation, a proclamation, which is being prepared even as I speak, will be signed and put into motion in the morning. That proclamation will call for an immediate emergency session of the General Assembly. We will ask the members of the Arkansas House and Senate to convene on Wednesday morning at ten o'clock for the purpose of initiating the process of impeachment and, ultimately, the removal from office of Jim Guy Tucker as governor of Arkansas.

My friends, let me tell you that this is one of the most painful decisions that I have ever had to make in my life. I do this with no pleasure. I do this without a sense of what politics may be involved. I do it because I have an awesome responsibility to you—the people who elected me and even the ones who did not —to do what I said I would do, and that is to uphold the Constitution of this state and of the United States.

When the founding fathers created our system of constitutional government, the genius of it was that we could change governments, entire governments, if not governors, without firing one shot, without one drop of blood, without one bomb, without a bullet, without bloodshed whatsoever. We must preserve the idea that our government is to be operated in the most honorable way, where we act not in our own best interest nor act in the best interest of our own political careers. We must—the people deserve it, the people demand it—we must act for what is best for our state and for those who have given us the sacred trust of public office. That is why, my friends, that I come to you with this sad news.

I hope the governor will, in fact, reconsider his decision today to withhold the resignation that he promised the people. Going back on one's word is a serious thing. I think that all of us can feel a sense of sadness and not joy, and yet a sense of resolve and, yes, a sense of community that we must and we will stand forth true, clear, and tall in this battle. If there are court challenges, let them come. We are more than ready to face them. If there are challenges of those who like to write columns or make opinions, let them come. We have not been elected to take a poll or to somehow check with opinion writers or to even be threatened by the possibility of legal action. We have been elected to serve you and to represent you.

I want to again say how much I appreciate all of the members of the General Assembly to a person. If there are any exceptions, I have not heard from them yet. But to a person, Democrats, Republicans alike, they have made it very clear that this is no time for us to draw sides. This is a time to draw together. And with Speaker Hogue, Senator Russ, their leadership, their wisdom, their experience, their commitment to joining with me in this unfortunate, unpleasant, painful, yet necessary action, we will show not only the people of Arkansas, but we will show the people of America that in this state we still believe in some old-fashioned values, in doing what is right. Whether it is good for us or not, whether it is good for our party or not, we want to do the right thing because we owe the people no less.

Several years ago, I lived in Pine Bluff. A dear friend and mentor of mine was longtime and now the late county judge, Earl Chadick. He was a grand old man. I will never forget Judge Chadick had in his office in the Jefferson County Courthouse a wonderful sign behind his desk. It simply said, "Come, let us reason together." That is how good government is supposed to work, and I am going to make sure that everyone of us, who can and will, remember that very thought. We will come. We will reason together.

It is my sincere prayer—and I mean this from the depths of my heart—it is my hope and prayer that Mr. Tucker will in fact have to my desk at nine o'clock in the morning a letter of resignation in which there are no qualifications. No ifs, ands, or buts. But if not, we will be fully prepared and will with resolve carry out the only thing that we can carry out, and that is the process of impeachment and then removal from office; and then, hopefully and finally, bring closure to this open and oozing wound. Not to the Democrats but to all of Arkansas.

My thanks to everyone of you as citizens who have been patient today—who came today expecting to be a part of a particular ceremony that perhaps you thought would mark a day in history. Instead, we have marked another kind of day in history. And tomorrow, it will be yet another moment of perhaps promise.

But here is what I pledge to you. I will make my share of mistakes. Always have. Always will. That is why I am grateful to God that he is a God who looks at us, and with all He knows about us, still loves us, still forgives, still empowers us to go on. Now there are those who tell me, "Mike, don't make so many quotes from the Bible in your speeches." Well, a word to those who, perhaps with good intentions, tell me not to reference God or the Bible. The fact is, since my childhood that Book and its Author have been the guiding forces of my life, and it would be much easier for me to give up being governor than it would be to give up taking the counsel that I have had from God and His Word.

Now I very much hope and trust that each one of you Arkansas citizens will let your desires be known to your state representative and state senator. You elected them to represent you, and I believe that these honorable men and women will. Don't think that the Democratic representatives don't feel equally embarrassed. Don't think that they have some agenda here other than what is best for Arkansas. Call them. Let them know tonight and tomorrow your feelings and desires, and let us all pray that Governor Tucker will do the right thing for Arkansas, for the Tuckers, and for Arkansas' history.

Thank you for letting me join with you. My wife Janet and I express sincere thanks for your prayers and your concerns and your love. And now, simply let me express to you that we want

America to see the best that we are and come to understand that Arkansas is truly a small but a wonderful, wonderful state with wonderful, wonderful people. God bless and good night.

Thirty minutes after this speech was broadcast, Governor Tucker's unconditional letter of resignation was received.

APPENDIX 4
THE PEOPLE'S BUSINESS

The inaugural address of Governor Mike Huckabee, delivered July 15, 1996, at about 7 p.m., five hours after it was originally scheduled and an hour after Governor Tucker's resignation.

As Yogi Berra might say, it seems like *deja vu* all over again! Folks, we have been through an exhausting and intense day, the likes of which perhaps has never happened in the halls of this Capitol. We have also been through a day that, I believe, will forever be remembered as a day in which people set aside everything regarding their political parties and stood together to act in the best interest of the state of Arkansas. Thank you.

Let no one say that today was a Republican victory, because it was not. Let no one say that it was Democrat embarrassment, because it was not. Let today be remembered as a day on which the people of Arkansas were the winners. All of us who stood together, who stood tall, can go back to our homes, to our families. And every one of you in this General Assembly, all the senators and the representatives, can go back and stand proudly to say that, in a moment which was perhaps as difficult for you as it has ever been serving in this body, you stood and did what you knew in your heart was right. The people of Arkansas, I believe, join me in expressing sincere thanks.

I want especially to single out Speaker Bobby Hogue, Senate President Pro Tempore Stanley Russ, Wayne Wagner, and many other members of the General Assembly, who took initiative, who took leadership positions today to give me a new hope about what's ahead for us as an Arkansas family.

Many have been speculating about what will happen when Mike Huckabee goes in and all the legislators are of the other party. Many have said that there's no way that a Republican governor can successfully work with members of a legislative body which is overwhelmingly of the other party. There have been all kinds of columns written and opinions expressed and views bantered in the halls of this marble building that what was ahead was gridlock, what was ahead would be all kind of heads crashing together. I think if we ever in our lives have done something to give the people of Arkansas a moment of great pride, it is today when we show the people of Arkansas what can and what will happen when we gather in this building to do, not our personal business, not our party's business, but when we gather to do the people's business.

My hat is off to every single Democrat as well as Republican legislator today, with a sincere hope that this is simply a sign to the people of our state that when they want to know what kind of working relationship we will have together, let's point them to the 15th of July 1996, and let's say, "That's what we did, and that's what we will, because that's what is right for Arkansas." We all, 135 members of this assembly and your governor, stand clear and are unapologetic for that idea. We must bring good government to the people, and today you have proven, as a General Assembly, that very thing.

I thank you. I tell you that the people of Arkansas thank you, and I hope that we'll be able to work like this now and as long as I happen to occupy my chair, which, after today, I realize could come and go at any moment. And as long as you occupy your chairs, I want everyone to understand that this would not have happened had it not been for the unity and for the show of support that I received from the speaker and the president pro tempore and other distinguished members of this body. And gentlemen, I could not be prouder than I am right now to say I serve with you; I serve for the people in the same capacity you do. And as we begin a new day in Arkansas history, a day we really didn't anticipate quite like this, I do so not with a sense of pessimism, but with a genuine, heartfelt sense of optimism.

There is a verse in the New Testament that says, "All things work together for good" (Rom. 8:28). I've often been reminded that it doesn't say all things are good. Some things aren't, but if we are patient, if we're kind, if we deeply seek out what we believe to be the right thing to do and stick with it, it is true that all things ultimately work together for good. Today, what I think has happened is that amidst all kinds of confusion and all kinds of scattered opinions and tension, the people of Arkansas now can look in on this chamber and the one on the other end of the hall and, I hope, the governor's office as well, and say, "We elected those people to remember us, and they did it; and we're grateful, we're proud, and we want them to show us more." That's how to make Arkansas an even better state—and that's tough to do because it's already the best there is!

Let me express a word that I hope you will understand needs to be said tonight. I, for one, am grateful, genuinely grateful, that in the last moments, Governor Tucker did, in fact, choose to do what was best for the state and make the decision to step aside, and to do it without qualification.

I know it was a painful decision for him. I recognize that it was something perhaps none of us, unless we have walked in his shoes, could have understood. All of us would probably want to be bitter, perhaps take offense, maybe even look back with some kind of scathing spirit. But my friends, I don't know what possibly could be gained by that. What had to be done today was done. The result is that we're gathered here, and that you have a new governor, prepared tomorrow to go to work with you and for you.

What we also have is one who did serve admirably. I really hope that in days that will come, we all will be able to remember him for what he did right, and not only circle around him the things which we believe he did wrong. That is to our credit if we do it. It is to our shame if we don't. I ask that we put aside every bit of malice, every bit of hurt or hard feelings, for it has no purpose; it has no place, and it really adds nothing except attention that, frankly, I think today we've proven we not only can live without, but when we do live without, we are able to offer up to the people of our great and wonderful state the kind of government that they can say, "I trust it. I believe in it."

There is a lot of cynicism about government. We all feel it. We all understand it. We all hear about it. This is our opportunity to stand in the way and to face all the criticism and the cynicism and to say good government is alive and well in Arkansas again. It's not Republican government. It's not Democrat government. It's just good government for the people.

I put my hand forth to each of you today with the sincere desire that you will join me in that kind of spirit and in singular commitment to the people of our state. Let's absolutely surprise them in the coming months, just as all of us have been surprised today. But let's surprise them with what good government can and will be when we decide that we love Arkansas a lot more than we do any label. The labels come and go, but we're Arkansas to the bone. Thank you, and God bless you!

APPENDIX 5
THE ARTS: A LIFETIME
OF LEARNING

During the 2004 National Forum on Education Policy, Arkansas Governor Mike Huckabee became chairman of the Education Commission of the States (ECS). In a speech delivered July 15, 2004, in Orlando, Florida, to a group of policymakers and education leaders from across the country, Huckabee outlined a new initiative—"The Arts: A Lifetime of Learning"—which was the centerpiece of his two years as ECS chairman.

All of you are aware that the theme for my initiative as ECS Chairman will be "The Arts: A Lifetime of Learning." This is a passion for me, not just a program, and you will see this over the next two years. I want to explain, on a very personal level, why this issue is so important to me.

The Old State House Museum in Little Rock is one you may have seen when Bill Clinton first announced his intent to run for President and when he accepted the presidency the night of his election in 1992. This museum has quite a bit of visibility in our state and across the world, as well. Inside there are many artifacts of Arkansas history and wonderful exhibits, both changing and stationary.

If you wandered up to the second floor of the museum, you would see something that might strike you at first as a bit unusual. You would see an old guitar in one of the glass cases. If you know anything about guitars, you might not think it to be all that impressive, since it's not very nice or expensive. You might even learn that the guitar is, in fact, a very *inexpensive* one. It was purchased in 1966 at a cost of $99, which included the electric guitar, the plastic case and the amplifier—the whole works—from the J.C. Penney catalog. You might wonder why that guitar is there. It's there because it happens to be the first guitar of a child who wanted to play so badly, his parents made an extraordinary sacrifice by scraping together $99 and purchasing it for this child's eleventh Christmas.

Like so many children who grew up in the era of the post-Beatles phenomenon, this kid learned to play the guitar, and played it so much that sometimes his fingers would almost bleed. Also like so many others, he never made it to the big time, never became a musician of renown. So why is his guitar in a museum?

It is on display because it belonged to me. In fact, the guitar is part of an exhibit of the First Families of Arkansas. Various governors donated artifacts from their childhoods and their lives, and this happened to be the first guitar I ever owned. I've owned quite a few since, most of which—thank goodness—are of a little better quality, but this guitar is priceless to me because it was my introduction to music. My parents thought it was noise, but by gosh, the music sounded good to me.

If you're wondering whether or not I've improved any since 1966, you'll have a chance to find out later during this conference when you hear the band I formed called Capitol Offense. I hope you will bring your dancing shoes, because we are not a concert band but rather a band that wants you to have a good time.

Our band opened this year for Willie Nelson in a sold-out arena concert of 8,000 people. We opened last year for the Charlie Daniels Band and have also worked with Dionne Warwick. A week from now we will be playing a concert with Grand Funk Railroad and later this year with 38 Special. We played one of the President's inaugural parties, and as of tomorrow night, we will have played all three Peabody Hotels—Orlando, Memphis, and Little Rock. We've played for the Southern Governors Association and for the Council of State Governments and in a host of other places where I find a way to get us invited because nobody else will have us.

My point in all of this is: participating in the arts is something I am still able to do. We may not be that sophisticated, since we're a classic rock-and-roll band, but we have a whole lot of fun and don't take ourselves too seriously. I will tell you something else as well: if I had been a great athlete in high school, played tackle football or the like, I would not be playing tackle football at my age now. However, I can still make music today. And ten, twenty or thirty years from now, I will still be able to make music. Just like Willie Nelson. When we played with him, I sat there in amazement and watched this seventy-year old man playing with the dexterity of a twenty-five-year old, making music and causing kids young enough to be his grandchildren to rush up to the front of the stage to greet him. I could not believe that this seventy-year old man is still making incredible music and enthralling crowds. It was so wonderful to see.

Over the next two years of my chairmanship at the Education Commission of the States (ECS), we are going to focus on learning, enjoying, and participating in the arts. Let me explain in a simple way the three main components of my initiative.

1) First of all, I want to be able to present what I call a case for the arts. A great deal of research supports the direct connection between arts education and academic improvement. Whether one looks at studies of students' ACT and SAT scores, or their math scores, or their capacity for learning foreign language, a tremendous body of evidence indicates a correlation between arts and academics as kids develop both the left and right sides of their brains. Through the arts, children are able to increase their capacity for spatial reasoning and their ability to think creatively.

Now some would say, "Well, I'm not too sure those studies are conclusive." Let's assume for the moment that they are not. Even so, participation in and appreciation of the arts can last a lifetime. Music, for example, is a life skill—an interest and an aptitude that one can maintain throughout a lifetime, unlike some interests that a kid will pick up and maybe never use again. It's not just about learning music or enjoying music, but participating in music. It can captivate a student.

A child can experience music at five or six or seven years old and spend the rest of his or her life developing a love and appreciation for it. That child will never outgrow it, and will never come to the place where he says, "It no longer can or should be a part of my life."

The benefits are too numerous to mention here, but one significant consequence of participating in the arts is that children learn teamwork. Imagine a child in the band who realizes his instrument may not be the loudest—it may not even be the one playing the primary melody—but when the conductor calls for that one moment when this child can shine, it's meaningful.

This kid learns something about life, doesn't he? A person in a musical group or a choir or a play understands that for every minute of performance, there are hours and hours and hours of practice. And that is how one gets good at anything.

Whether it's being in the band or being the CEO of a major company, the life lessons learned by participating in the arts are clearly invaluable.

In fact, one survey of CEOs across America determined that the common denominator of successful CEOs was not that they were the valedictorians of their class or even in the top 10 percent academically. The common denominator was their participation in team activities as they were growing up. Such activities taught them both to lead and to follow and to be part of a group.

To put it simply, we need to focus on the arts in education because the arts teach kids how to learn. Through the arts, children are presented with huge amounts of new information they can process and use to participate in activities they enjoy. Through the arts, children develop creative skills which carry them toward new ideas, new experiences and new challenges, not to mention a great deal of satisfaction. This is the intrinsic value of the arts, and it cannot be overestimated in any way.

2) The second component of my ECS initiative is to establish a place for the arts. That place ought to be our schools, where children already are gathered and are learning. Ensuring that arts education is part of every school will not only enhance student achievement, it will give children access to activities and interests that will benefit and enrich their lives.

I get really angry when I hear people speak of the arts as if it is only an extracurricular, extraneous, and expendable endeavor in our schools. Let me tell you, I think it is an essential part of an overall well-rounded education. If we are not providing an arts education, including music, the visual arts, theater, dance and more, then we are not doing enough. It is critical to touch the talent of every kid, no matter what that talent is. And in far too many of our schools, we have been willing to touch the talent as long as it's about running fast, jumping high, or throwing a ball better than another kid.

I enjoy sports, too, and these skills are wonderful, but I also know that many of those kids who play sports and who are proud of their letter jackets when they are seniors in high school will find those jackets hanging in their closets by the time they are twenty-five. For most students, sports alone will not propel them to the next level of success in life. They won't be able to play or participate for life, but rather will only be able to be spectators. The arts, however, can build skills and appreciation that can be used and enjoyed for a lifetime.

I think we need a place for both arts and athletics in our schools—in that order, frankly. We need a place for every student in every school in America to find his or her talent in the arts.

3) The third component of my chairman's initiative is to put a face on the arts. Let me personalize this by giving you some examples of famous Arkansans who have parlayed their participation in the arts from poverty to prosperity.

One of the great entertainers of all time, Johnny Cash, grew up as one of the poorest kids in Arkansas in a little bitty community called Kingsland. Johnny Cash lived there until he was three when his family moved to northeast Arkansas and tried to farm as best they could. There, not far from Memphis, he heard sounds that ranged from gospel and blues to country. Out of all those experiences and sounds, he put together his own unique styling, found his way to Sam Phillips' Sun recording studios in Memphis, and joined up with a band called the Tennessee Three. The rest, as they say, is history, and Johnny Cash made plenty of it in the music industry. He became a crossover artist of great success who was respected in virtually every genre of music. This is just one example of a kid who truly found himself through the arts and will leave a legacy on society because of his music and his personal artistry.

Another example is Mary Steenburgen, whose father was a railroad worker in northern Little Rock, Arkansas. She came from a working-class family and now, as you know, is an Oscar-winning actress.

Billy Bob Thornton, who grew up in Malvern, Arkansas, is a brilliant writer, actor, and director. But he did not grow up in the way that he lives now. He grew up the son of a local high school coach and a psychic. Although he battled undesirable circumstances like the loss of his father as a teen, he was able to parlay the dreams that were burning within him to become a successful writer, producer, actor, and Oscar winner.

I present these examples, not because somebody might be the next Johnny Cash or Billy Bob Thornton or Mary Steenburgen, but to point out that there is a kid who will play in the high school band and will learn how to play the trumpet. Prior to learning the trumpet, this kid will have no place. He won't be a great basketball player or be picked for the team at recess. But one day, somebody will put a trumpet in his hands, and he will find his gift from God. When he plays, he not only will find the blessing within himself, but people who have never given him attention before will give him their applause.

For every one of you in this room today who has ever heard applause for something that you did and did well, I don't have to tell you that self-esteem is not the result of somebody saying, "Here, here is your self-esteem. Go feel better about yourself." It is the result of being allowed to be good at what you are gifted to do. Then self-esteem takes care of itself.

Don't we owe that opportunity to every kid in America? Don't we owe to every child, whether his talent is basketball or the tuba, the ability to experience it? The face of the arts should be the face that we hope to see on every kid as he walks out on a stage. The face may be playing only a tiny part in a play, but that child knows that the hours of practice meant something. The lines memorized or the instrument learned or the song written all mean something, and that child can feel good about his efforts and achievement.

Placed around this room is artwork that has been brought to us by the Créalde School of Art. In looking at this work, I have a great sense of joy knowing that a child, somewhere, took a blank board and created something that represented his thoughts, his spirit, and his heart.

Inside every human being, there are secrets to unlock and treasures to unlatch. We owe it to all children to make sure that whatever their talent happens to be—theater, music, dance, or painting—doors are open for them. We must make sure that they don't go through life without ever discovering their talents.

If education means anything, it means that we as educational leaders build bridges and open doors. All education ultimately does this. The best piece of advice I ever received came from a gentleman in my hometown who said to me, as I was getting ready to go to college, "Now Mike, I hope you don't think that when you get to college, they're going to teach you everything you need to know, because they can't. In fact, if you approach it that way, you are going to be miserably unhappy for the rest of your life with what college does for you." (He wanted to tell me these things because he knew I would be the first generation in my family to ever go to college.) He went on, "Just remember this: college won't teach you what you need to learn for life. All that college and education can do is to help you to learn *how* to learn. You will spend the rest of your life as a student, and you will never quit learning. If you learn that in college, it will be a great experience for you."

Wouldn't it be wonderful today if, through the Education Commission of the States, we could awaken a national sense of priority for the arts, a national sense of appreciation and participation in all fifty states? Wouldn't it also be wonderful to turn up the volume on the arts and make sure that we use the megaphone of this organization to say to every governor, to every state school chief, to every superintendent, to every school board member, to every parent in every district in this country, that we will insist that every child have the opportunity to learn, enjoy and participate in the arts?

I hope you will join me over the next two years in these efforts, so that two years from now we will look back and say that we have not just changed the attitudes about curriculum, but we have changed the future of America by building bridges and opening doors. Every kid in America is going to have access to the arts. I look forward to working with you, and I thank you very much.

APPENDIX 6
WELCOME, NEIGHBORS:
LIFE AFTER KATRINA

Governor Huckabee's speech in Little Rock after 75,000 victims of Hurricane Katrina sought refuge in Arkansas. This speech was delivered August 31, 2005.

It has been a pleasure and a privilege to welcome our neighbors from the Gulf whose lives have been upended by Hurricane Katrina. I couldn't have made the commitments I did, unless I knew that all Arkansans were standing shoulder-to-shoulder with me, waiting to help, wanting to help. Your overwhelming generosity has been surpassed only by our guests' overwhelming gratitude.

In a way, we all live below sea level, hoping that the levees we have built will hold and protect us. Yet inevitably, the storms come and our façades crumble, sunken by a parent's Alzheimer's, a spouse's alcoholism, a daughter's leukemia, a son's drug addiction. We looked at the victims and saw ourselves, because we have all spent long days and nights in our own version of that overpass on Interstate 10. All of us remember those who lifted us on their backs and carried us to higher ground. We jumped at the chance to repay their kindness and comfort.

While hard work lies ahead, the worst of this crisis is now behind us. The most agonizing, frustrating part was when we were sitting helplessly, wringing our hands, seeing suffering survivors, yet being unable to reach them. During those awful first few days, so many of us thankfully fed our children and put them to bed, But seeing the hungry, we couldn't eat; seeing the sleepless, we couldn't rest. We watched TV most of the night, keeping a vigil with them, praying with them. We were as bewildered and shocked as they were that this could be happening in our country.

Now we can throw our arms around them. Now we can roll up our sleeves and make ourselves useful.

The symbolism isn't lost on me that many folks are staying in church camps because, while it is wonderful to study God's Word, it is even better to live it. Our guests tell me how lucky they are to be here, but we, their hosts, are the lucky ones to have this opportunity to serve. They thank me for visiting with them, but being with them gives me so much more than I could ever hope to give them. Thank you for the opportunity to share your stories, your faith, your love, your optimism. Thank you for reminding us that life is precious, and that everything else, we can either replace or do without. In his poem "Success," Ralph Waldo Emerson wrote, ". . . to know that even one life has breathed easier because you have lived." Today, we are making tens of thousand of lives breathe easier.

Hard work lies ahead, not just in caring for the victims and rebuilding their communities, but in evaluating what went wrong at all levels of government. Four years after 9/11, with our new Department of Homeland Security, with our new National Response Plan, we thought we were much better prepared for those twin threats without conscience or mercy—Al Qaeda and Mother Nature. We thought that when we called in the cavalry, we would hear bugles blaring and hooves pounding. Katrina has shown us that we must go back to the drawing board.

Congress is investigating, the White House is investigating, but the governors must also investigate from our perspective, since we are literally in the middle of all disaster response between the local and federal authorities. As chairman of the National Governor's Association, I will lead the other governors in reviewing what we expect from our local governments, what they expect from us, and what we expect from FEMA and the Department of Homeland Security. We must fill the gaps, and we must clear up the misunderstandings. The failure here was not one of resources, not a lack of bottled water or blankets or generators or helicopters. It was a failure of leadership, of imagination. It was not, as some have falsely tried to paint it, a failure of compassion and concern, but of command and control.

Especially in New Orleans, we were never on top of this crisis. We were like Tantalus in the Greek myth, neck-deep in water with fruit trees hanging over him. When he tried to drink, the water receded. When he tried to reach a piece of fruit, the wind blew the branches away. He was condemned by the gods to spend eternity with food and water "tantalizingly" close but always just beyond his grasp. However hard we tried to grasp the crisis that first week—a week that felt like an eternity—it kept getting away from us.

If you fail to complete a crucial step in your emergency response plan, then you have to scramble to meet the changed circumstances. You have to think on your feet. You have to be calm, clear-headed, and creative under tremendous pressure. The plan in place called for New Orleans to be evacuated, with buses to take out those who didn't have their own transportation. The plan envisioned relief operations—food, shelter, and medical care—outside the city. But with so many people left *inside* New Orleans, the plan was no longer viable.

Relief outside a city suddenly had to become relief and rescue inside a submerged city—a far more arduous undertaking. Instead of getting supplies in to tide folks over while the initial rescue was going on, focusing on the young and the old, the sick and the injured, there was only paralysis and confusion. There was neither relief nor rescue. As the waters rose, no government entity, no leader rose to the challenge. People drowned—literally—in bureaucracy. They ended up in a pine box because of a failure to think outside the box.

Just before Katrina hit, with the fourth anniversary of 9/11 approaching, I was regretting how the unity we felt right after the attacks had faded. I was wishing that we could somehow recapture that spirit the way our children catch fireflies in a jar. We had gone back to being Red States and Blue States, North and South, Coasts and Heartland. But Katrina once again stripped away our superficial differences and our petty rivalries, and brought us back to our most meaningful, core identity: we are Americans. Despite the vastness of this country, in times of crisis we are a small town; we are caring neighbors. We speak with different accents but with one voice, a voice that asks, "How can I help?"

Besides uniting us as Americans, Katrina reminded us of our common humanity. We smugly pride ourselves on being so "advanced," so "civilized" compared to many Third World countries. We believe we are hundreds of years ahead of them. But really, we are just a day away from joining them. We are not so different from them after all. Our high technology and our complex infrastructure exists and functions subject to the whims of nature, of elements as basic as wind and water.

Islamic terrorism didn't begin on 9/11, but it took 9/11 to make us wake up and face it head-on. Persistent poverty didn't begin with Katrina, but it has taken Katrina to wake us up to face it head-on. The difference between being poor and being middle class—the ability to load up your car and use your credit card to buy gasoline and a motel room—was in many cases the difference between who lived and who died. These are folks who have spent their whole lives trying to keep their heads above water, and it was only when their figurative struggle became a reality that they got our attention. These are folks who were left behind when the diplomas were given out, when the good jobs were given out. And when Katrina came, they were left behind yet again. We cringe with shame looking back on the days when African-Americans had to ride in the back of the bus. But this time, they didn't even have buses to board. Many of Katrina's victims follow in the footsteps of those martyred in the civil rights movement—those who died bringing attention to their plight, so that their brothers and sisters would have a better life.

While we must have a safety net for those who suffer temporary setbacks or are too disabled to work, if you cast that net too wide, then healthy, capable Americans become caught and tangled and never achieve their potential. Those who believe in a permanent underclass are defeatists and racists. If you truly care about people, you don't write off their ability to take care of themselves. You don't pay them off not to contribute to society. You don't consign them to a subsistence-level standard of living. You don't exile them to the plantations of public housing, generation after generation. You include them. You offer them the excitement of learning, the challenge of job training, the dignity of a hard-earned paycheck, so that instead of being stuck in a nightmare of dependency and hopelessness, they get back on track to share the American dream. That is the promise we should make to the victims of Katrina, living and dead.

Fifty years from now, I want the children of Katrina to tell their grandchildren how suddenly everything was gone. There was no food or water, no bed to sleep in, no toys to play with. The days were very hot and the nights were very scary. And then they came to Arkansas, and the people gave them everything they needed and much more. I want them to say that their time in Arkansas was one of the blessings of their lives.

And fifty years from now, I want the children of Arkansas to tell their grandchildren how suddenly strangers arrived with nothing, but how they and their parents shared what they had, and made each sad, crying stranger smile again.

I hope that many of our guests will feel so at home among us that they will decide to stay. But I know that for most, the pull of home will be too powerful, and you will return when you can. Whether you stay or not, today you are Arkansans—you will *always* be Arkansans—and we open our homes and hearts, our schools and churches, our parks and playing fields to you. Give us a chance: we'll learn to cook a great gumbo.